T0383726

MAVERICK MAESTRO

MAVERICK MAESTRO

MAURICE PERESS

Routledge
Taylor & Francis Group
LONDON AND NEW YORK

First published 2015 by Paradigm Publishers

Published 2016 by Routledge
2 Park Square, Milton Park, Abingdon, Oxon OX14 4RN
711 Third Avenue, New York, NY 10017, USA

*Routledge is an imprint of the Taylor & Francis Group,
an informa business*

Library of Congress Cataloging-in-Publication Data

Peress, Maurice.
    Maverick maestro / Maurice Peress.
        pages cm.— (Nine lives musical series)
    ISBN 978-1-61205-874-0 (hardcover : alk. paper)—
    ISBN 978-1-61205-876-4 (library ebook)—
    ISBN 978-1-61205-877-1 (consumer ebook)
    1. Peress, Maurice. 2. Conductors (Music)—United States—
Biography. I. Title.
    ML422.P464A3 2015
    780.92—dc23
    [B]
                                                    2014042162

ISBN 13: 978-1-61205-874-0 (hbk)
ISBN 13: 978-1-61205-875-7 (pbk)

Contents

Foreword

*A*s all of you will find when you read *Maverick Maestro*, you are drawn into such a rich life and enter into so many worlds, you feel that you are watching a great movie you wish would never end.

The author's extraordinary life story and his journeys through 84 years of nonstop searching and achieving makes you feel that you are living these adventures with him. Maurice Peress's honesty and idealism fill every page of this book, providing us all a desperately needed breath of fresh air, reminding us that we must follow our hearts to have a meaningful life.

This is the kind of biography of an American artist that every musician and artist of any genre would dream of having written about them someday. Maurice Peress made that dream a reality by writing it himself, creating a riveting account of all the lives he has lived and portraits of the lives of so many other people whom we now feel that we also know.

A word of caution. Don't read this book if you think that you can put it down or read it in installments. Once you start, you can't stop until the end, and when you reach the final two words,

THE END, it seems that no time has gone by. It took me seven hours to read it from cover to cover, and I am eagerly awaiting the sequel, but in the meantime, will re-read it again.

This book will not only be a lifetime guide for everyone who wants a life in music. it will be an invaluable addition for students of sociology, American studies, urban studies, comparative religions, theater, films, and all the arts. *Maverick Maestro* is a perfect work for today's young artists of all genres to show that the greatest career in life any of us can attain is being able to work tirelessly in order to make a contribution while we are here. Maurice Peress has done that and is still doing it every day, and his book is a celebration of the creative spirit and the joy that music brings to us all when we decide to serve and honor it.

Bravo Maestro.

David Amram
Beacon, NY
September 2014

Acknowledgments

*A*s I was reading the galleys of this memoir, the news of the passing of Manuela Kruger, my friend and editor, the book's "without whom," struck. My first thanks and dedication goes to Manuela. I want to also recognize Kate Bowen Gill, who asked the key question that eventually shaped my book, "What distinguishes your musical career?" I have learned so much from my students and fellow musicians, and the mysterious embrace of the art we serve. This is their book as well. And infinite thanks to Dave Amram who introduced me to the intrepid Dean Birkenkamp, who makes Paradigm Publishers possible.

Prologue

Late August 2014 in New York: Time lingers—

Like a kid late for school, I grab my portfolio with the score for Bernstein's *Mass* and take a look in the front hall mirror to adjust my beret before heading out the door. I smile at the man with a white beard who smiles back at me and greet myself—"Maestro of Flushing"—the moniker the *New York Times* gave me in an article a few years ago. I'll take it!

Driving over the Triborough Bridge to rehearse in Flushing, with Manhattan glittering in the early morning: Let's face it. It has been forty-three years since I conducted the premiere of *Mass*. What did I know? Everything! My proudest moment. What have I learned? I am much more in awe now, more humble and thankful for my gifts than I ever was as an arrogant forty-one-year-old. Who gets to do this? Who gets to be a maestro—whether in New York City, Corpus Christi, or Kansas City ... or Flushing? How does that happen?

As in all cases there were no magic beans or fairy godmothers, but I have to confess my life does seem to be a little magical—or is the word simply blessed, *beshert* as they say in Yiddish? How does a firstborn son of Jewish immigrants from Washington Heights who decides *not* to take over the family business and plays jazz trumpet instead end up conducting opening night at the Kennedy Center—or a symphony orchestra in Vienna, or an Ellington premiere in Chicago?

I want to tell my story. And because my career as a conductor unfolded in such an atypical way, I title this memoir *Maverick Maestro*.

I

Beginnings

♪

*H*ow to portray the events of my formative years? They can be trotted out in neat linear fashion, but in fact they overlap in complex ways. What remains is brain-like, a glob of experiences that cannot simply be peeled away layer by layer, but is ever expanding and contracting, exuding ideas and talents and contradictions that have carried me through life, that carry me still.

There are my immigrant parents from long-separated Judaic worlds making a new life in America. There is music, deeply held in my dad's heart and passed on to me. And my happy time of discovery in the 1930s with radio, science, music, and sports. And the family store, our face before the world, until it all was interrupted by war and the Holocaust that swallowed up my mother's family and dislodged my dad's. There was above all a sense of justice unfulfilled, and a mission emerged: find a way to use music to serve the greater good.

My split world was in evidence from the very beginning, in my naming. Both my grandfathers were named after the Old

Testament patriarch Moses—Dad's dad was Moshi and Mom's dad, Moshe. Moshi died just before my birth. And in the ancient tradition of so many cultures for perpetuating a grand old name through the generations, Dad wanted his firstborn to be named Moshi Heskel-Ezra Peress, a patronymic embracing four generations. There was a time when names were strung out even longer. The sons and grandsons of our "Ur" ancestor, a man named Joseph Horesh—possibly Hirsch, who left Vienna for Baghdad ca. 1710, a name that still appeared on the Turkish tax list of 1892—dropped all but their given names, one of them being the first Peres, a biblical name from Genesis 38:27.

Mother objected. Following her Ashkenazi tradition she believed it would be bad luck to name me Moshi while her father lived. And the standoff continued until my eighth day of life, March 26, 1930, when the mohel, the ritual circumciser, suggested a compromise Hebrew name, Menasha. They had already agreed that my American name would be Maurice. One of several explanations to myself for my father's distancing himself from me is the disappointment and shame he must have felt not being able to honor his late father through his firstborn son. As my psychiatrist later pointed out, we cannot compare Moses with Menasha, a minor member of one of the twelve tribes.

We leap ahead four decades to start our story on September 8, 1971, the musical high point of my life, conducting the world premiere of Leonard Bernstein's *Mass* for the inauguration of the John F. Kennedy Center for the Performing Arts in Washington, DC.

In the Opera House center box sits my wife, Gloria Vando; Rose Kennedy; and the composer. I am in the pit.

With one stroke of his guitar, Allen Titus, the Celebrant, wipes away the cacophonous *Kyries* pouring out of speakers from the four corners of the Opera House. "Sing God a simple song," he implores. The orchestra enters—a whisper. We are aloft, releasing the essence imprisoned in cold printed notes, alive in a universe of sound. I keep the whole quivering mass flowing together, responding instantly to any slight discoordination, pressing into or stretching climaxes, lingering on edges of calm ... as if guiding my child safely and gratifyingly through the waved sea for the first time. I am also instinctively aware of the audience: the absolute silence and shallow breathing when they are locked onto the lifeline of drama and sound, urging us on, or, God forbid, when they are restless and we have to win them back.

All of Bernstein's finales are bigger-than-life love-ins, paeans to brotherhood, to the possibility of a better world to come. As the last *amen* of the chorale "Bless This House and All Who Gather Here," and Lenny's voice, a benediction, "Go in Peace," fade away, a rainbow of choristers and clarinetists, drummers and dancers, floods the stage; the audience, sharing the grief of a cast now in tears, is on their feet. This congregation, this *mass* of people, finds itself waking up in the House of John F. Kennedy. In seconds I am onstage for bows. Lenny by my side whispers, "You can throw out your CV." And yes, a wider if curvy career road did lie before me, but I am mostly joyous with the accomplishment of bringing off a work so huge and complex ... and filled with wonder about the *affect* of *Mass*. Did Bernstein's message, our message, reach into the audience? Will the critics love us? Will this House sing forever? (See photographs 1 and 2.)

Music started with my dad, Heskel-Ezra Moshi Peress, born in Baghdad (date unknown, ca. 1902) into a large family of traders that can be traced back to the seventeenth century. "What did Grandpa Moshi do?" I asked. "He went to the souk every morning and bought and sold, mostly tobacco." After graduation from Alliance Israelite, one of several schools established by French intellectuals throughout the Middle East to educate Jewish men and women in the modern ways of Europe—the Babylonian Rabbinate were *not* happy—my dad-to-be had learned fluent French, Arabic, and Hebrew, and could scribe a formal letter in Victorian English. I have his English copybook, written in flowery script with a dip pen point and ink. In addition to proverbs and lists of a vocabulary useful in commerce, the copybook contains sample letters, among them a formal invitation: "Dear Captain read [*sic*], Will you favour Mrs. Knight and myself with your company at dinner on Monday next at six o'clock. We expect General Rawley and his wife, and think you may like to make their acquaintance. Believe me ... yours truly."

Dad found work as a clerk under the British, who ruled this slice of the former Ottoman Empire through their Mesopotamian Mandate, a prize of World War I. The "land between the rivers" now became Iraq. Dad drove a car throughout the countryside inspecting farms and writing reports on their condition. He must have been aware of the roiling tensions between the British and the Hashemite Muslims. Dad did tell me that once the new Arab ruler, King Faisal, took charge, non-Muslim clerks were slowly being let go, so it was just a matter of time before he might be as well.

By all reports he was happy in Iraq. He learned to play oud—the same soft-strumming *l'ud,* or lute, that the returning Crusaders brought back to Spain and France in the fifteenth century—and sang Arabic songs with unusual feeling and passion that placed him at the center of family parties, *challys,* like the ones I grew up with. He was often joined by his brother Sassoon on *k'noon,* a zither, and his father, Moshi, on *dumbek,* an hourglass drum. With his buddies (contacts with women outside the immediate family were not allowed) he swam the Tigris after flood season and picnicked on the newly verdant islands as they resurfaced. His prospects were few. He could follow the traditional family ways and wait his turn for an arranged marriage, with an accompanying dowry sufficient to support a business; or he could be brave and make a new life ... in America. He quietly applied for a visa just as the US Immigration Act of 1924 affixed a limit of one hundred visas per year for Iraqi citizens. He waited patiently, and in the summer of 1926, visa in hand, he told his family of his plans. There was much wailing and weeping, and promises were made—he would of course return for a proper marriage. By car and train and ferry he traveled through Aleppo, Alexandria, Bari, and to Cherbourg, where H. M. Peress, second-class passenger #259, boarded the USS *Leviathan* on August 10, 1926, and six days later landed at New York's Pier 86, at the foot of West 46th Street.

Dad found work behind the counter in linen shops owned by fellow Arabic-speakers. In 1927 he was selling hosiery in the Bronx when in walked Elka (Elsie) Frimit Tiger to buy a pair of silk hose. Elsie at age twenty-three was a tall, slender, full-figured beauty. (See photograph 3.) She spoke Yiddish and broken English. Elsie and her sister Lena had emigrated from a town near Warsaw four years earlier and lived in a walkup apartment on nearby

Hoe Avenue. They traveled each morning by the "elevated" to a sweatshop not far from Astor Place, where they worked as by-the-piece sewers of men's ties. Their weekly letters back to Poland always included a two-dollar bill.

The hosiery Elsie purchased soon started to "run" (as they were designed to), and she returned to complain to the dark man behind the counter. This oft-told tale never followed through on what was done about the torn stockings, but Heskel, by now Americanized to Henry, asked her for a date. "But I only go out with Jewish boys." Dad was prepared. From under the counter he pulled up a siddur, a Hebrew prayer book—for all I know it was the same one from Baghdad that he kept all his life and passed down to me along with his English copybook—and started to read to her in Hebrew, in an accent strange to Mom's ears I am sure, but it was Hebrew. "Ah," said she to herself, "he's one of those dark Jews" she'd heard about. Mom was a movie buff. Only a year earlier a swarthy Rudolph Valentino set hearts aflutter when he appeared in the *Sheik of Araby*, and here was one in the flesh! They were married in June 1928, and within two years I was born.

Mother always worked. There were eleven kids in Poland, born a year or two apart as can be expected for a healthy couple that lived by the book, the Torah and Talmud. Grandpa Moshe was a bespoke tailor. The store was also their home. Once weaned and walking, the kids no longer slept with their parents in the one bedroom next to the big coal stove but moved onto one of the cutting tables. They learned to sew before they could read: handmade buttonholes, cuffs and hems, how to set in a sleeve. In America Mother and her sister Lena earned their way sewing on treadle machines.

Dad came from a middle-class Babylonian family, from the land where the Talmud had been written; again there were nine children born a year or two apart. None of Dad's four sisters went to school. Girls were relegated to the kitchen and to raising children. His mother, Grandmama "Imy" Toba, arrived in America in her seventies and clever as she was, could only read numbers. Once I was born, Dad assumed Mom would stay at home with the baby, a strange creature he watched from afar; nor did he ever touch food except to eat it.

But as I said, Mom always worked. So this culture clash was resolved, for I have early memories of my mom alone in a small girdle and bra shop on Broadway and 171st Street. I must have been five or six. My chin did not reach the edge of the counter, but I could read numbers. I remember a customer coming in for a corset. "I wear a size 38," she announced. "I have just what you need," said Mama. "Why don't you go into the fitting room and undress and I will bring it to you to try on." I watched as Mother drew out a 34 from the shelf. I was mortified! She ran over to the Singer treadle sewing machine—bought for five dollars secondhand, to be sold decades later as an antique for fifty dollars—ripped open the garment, cut an inset out of pinkish cloth to fit, sewed it into place, and headed for the fitting room as she bit off the hanging ends of thread with her teeth. "Here, try this on." A pull, a tug, a few more adjustments, adding (again at the trusty Singer) "a piece plush" where it cut, or a longer stocking holder. Within minutes the customer left satisfied. Mama "made the sale." All's well.

Two things stand out from that time of innocence: my love of music and of nature. Dad was a man of few words. He worked long hours but on Sunday mornings he made magic happen. In his slippers and robe Dad sat with his oud on a low cassock amid deeply colored flowers and pomegranates woven into our Kashan carpet. He shaved a new tip at the end of his eagle-feather pick and curled it round his dark, hairy hand. Turning one ear to listen, he carefully tuned the single wire-wound bass note and four pairs of gut strings ... paused ... took an extra deep breath, and began to play and sing. Mysterious-sounding Arabic words I didn't understand mixed with the oud's gentle rhythms. Dad was transported outside of himself, as was I, his entire being given to the music, the notes, the sound. We were risen up together, two souls joining. This was my first real music. I learned to sing the Arabic songs "*S'heertu*" and "*Y'dunia e-egaramii*" that I have since learned are songs of pain and longing ("I lie awake through the night" and "My world is in pain"). I have no doubt that my becoming a musician—rather than the engineer I went to Brooklyn Tech to become—can be traced back to this closeness with Dad and his music. (See photograph 4.)

Washington Heights in the 1930s: The clops and tinkly rattle of the horse-drawn milk wagon signaled the end of night as it pulled to a stop on the street below. Next I would hear glassy clinks as bottles of milk were placed by the door of our apartment; their thick, waxy paper tops skirted tight by a soldered wire. We were careful to save the cream that floated above the milk for Dad's coffee. The milkman's sounds were soon joined by a rolling, roiling racket of steel on steel that arose from the Broadway trolley tracks a half block away, reminding me how the tough boys in the neighborhood could hitch rides on the rounded back of the trolley, hanging on to god-knows-what. I suffered envious disapproval: "Wouldn't it be grand to hitch, to be brave and reckless like the tough kids?" But already the line was drawn between the "Amsterdams" and the goody-goody kids like me who lived in the tenements west of Broadway.

Our first apartment, on the ground floor of 171st just west of Broadway, had a real icebox—I still call a refrigerator "icebox." Every few days the iceman "cameth" shouldering a huge sparkling cube on his leather chamois rag and he ice-picked it down to size for the upper cabinet. I'd get a splinter or two to suck on. For the next few days Mother would empty melted water that collected in the under-tray into the sink as the cube got smaller and smaller.

I loved my Mickey Mouse table radio and the bigger boxy one in the living room. On WOR every afternoon at five o'clock, "Uncle Don" told stories and sang songs: "A tree in the woods, and the woods in the ground, and the green grass grew all round and round." He would announce birthdays. And for children who were good there would be a present hidden behind the radio. On at least one March 18th I peeked in vain behind our radio hoping to find a birthday gift. There were the daily serials on WJZ and WEAF: *Jack Armstrong, The Shadow, The Lone Ranger, Flash Gordon*—each with musical signatures. On Saturday mornings I listened to *Let's Pretend.* Around age twelve I would mail away for tickets on a Monday morning and by Wednesday or Thursday a square beige envelope would arrive with two tickets for the Saturday show. Mail, quick and dependable, was delivered twice a day. We took the A train, transferred to the D, got off at Rockefeller Center station, and climbed tall stairs directly into the glorious art deco NBC building. A half century later I would be working for Duke Ellington in that same building.

On early spring mornings I would quietly slip out of the apartment and walk the empty dawn-lit streets to a nearby miniature park in the middle of Broadway, where a few budding trees and a small plot of grass surrounded a World War I field cannon with big frozen wheels. I brought along some breadcrumbs, and if I got there early enough, I would have an empty bench and a flock of pigeons all to myself. The low-lying sun soon rose over the tenements, taking the chill out of the morning air, letting me know it was time to walk back home for breakfast and school. I started reading books about botany, and a year later at summer camp I immediately joined the Nature Club and sewed a big green felt maple leaf onto my gray sleeveless camp shirt.

In 1936 Mom delivered my brother, Herbert—Hebrew name Herzl, after Theodore Herzl, founder of Zionism. I was getting over scarlet fever and was home in bed when the door flew open and Dad rushed in all excited and ran around the house chanting, "It's a boy, it's a boy, it's a boy." And again, "It's a boy, it's a boy, it's a boy." I jumped up, danced around on the bed, and gathered up all my gold and silver metallic toys into a tin pail, little hammers and chisels, and gave them to Dad to "help pay for the baby" before he rushed out.

Window trimming week in the big Peress Shop in Washington Heights: Samples were taken from stock; robes, slips, bras; ironed, and the prices listed on paper sheets saved from empty hosiery boxes. Mr. Krisch, Dad's longtime artistic window trimmer, would then draw the fancy price tickets with his special engraver's pen and India ink, soon to be strategically placed in the new window on or near the garments: "$3.98, Two for $7.89." Sometimes Dad would send me to scout a nearby competitor's window to see what they were charging for a particular item and we would lower our price by a penny! Coffee at the soda fountain next door was a nickel.

Meanwhile the old window displays had to be cleared. When I was old enough, Dad gave me over-socks for my shoes and I climbed in and helped undo the window; working from back to front, I carefully removed the merchandise, the old price tickets, and chrome-plated display stands, then passed out the goods that were to be returned to stock and readied the display stands for the new merchandise. The huge covered-plywood floor panels would be taken out last, stripped, and recovered by Mr. Krisch according to the season—yellow paper for summer, light brown for fall, white for winter, and green for spring. The floodlight gels were changed and replaced to enhance the color of a particular grouping. Boxes of trim and scatterings, beach sand or Christmas tinsel or fall leaves, would be brought up from the basement storage according to the season at hand. I now realize I was being introduced to stage lighting and design—decades later I watched in awe as the diva, Regina Resnik, walked the San Francisco Opera War Memorial stage to find the best-lit spots for her arias.

Mr. Krisch was ready to perform his magic. In his socks, he entered the window and called for the low-lying merchandise and arranged it artistically up front. Dad would go outside to approve or suggest changes as the window filled; the tall mannequin dolls (with those perfectly tilted breasts), dressed in a gown or bathing suit, brought up the rear and the completed window was sealed. We would all run out to see the final display and "ooh and aah."

And so, three-quarters of a century later my darling brother, Herbert, his own artistic director for Peress of Madison Avenue, sends us Internet shots of the new Christmas window, the gowns gleaming in the light for us to "ooh and aah" over.

Violin lessons: From my present state of musical sophistication the episode of my early fiddle lessons is funny and pathetic. I was eight or nine years old. The teacher came to the house once a week. I think he was subsidized by the WPA. He was paid thirty-five cents a lesson and that included the use of a three-quarter-size loaner fiddle. I remember meeting him at the door asking him to please tune it. Eventually I struggled with a four-whistle pitchpipe, but the fiddle was at best sourly tuned until the following week. When summer came and we moved to the seashore we did not take the violin with us. The following fall Mom heard that my piano-whiz schoolmate, Elliot Zuckerman, who lived on the floor above, got free lessons at the Henry Street Settlement House and decided we should apply. The violin was stored atop my dad's dark wood clothing cabinet we called a chifforobe. When I opened the case, one of the strings was broken and I told my mom I need that string for my piece.

So this is how it went. Mom telephoned with an impossible white lie: "Mister, we're on the trolley and my son forgot his violin. Can you lend us one when we get there?" They agreed and we arrived. I had my piece, my music, in hand. A young woman handed me a full-size violin, and I handed it back and asked her to tune it for me. I was escorted into a studio to play for the master teacher. I put my music on the stand and started to play "Hatik-vah," the Jewish national anthem. The teacher and his assistant, my trusty fiddle tuner, suppressed their laughter. I was escorted out and overheard the teacher (he was Jascha Heifetz's father!): "Mrs. Peress, I think you should stop wasting money on violin lessons." And she did.

I had a good ear and could sing in tune and found myself in two small vocal ensembles; at PS 173 I sang alto in a children's choir arrangement of the "Halleluiah Chorus" from Handel's *Messiah,* and with a vocal quartet in my Catholic Cub Scouts troop I sang Stephan Foster's "Beautiful Dreamer" and "Breathe and Blow, Breathe and Blow, Wind [pronounced Wynd] of the Western Sea." For a long time, this and singing in Hebrew for my bar mitzvah were the extent of my musical life.[1]

I contracted "Bugle Fever," became infatuated with the bugle, at thirteen. Its noble noise reached far and wide when I sounded it at sleep-away Camp Everett in the Berkshires. Power! Everyone had to respond when I played "ya-gotta-get-up, ya-gotta-get-up" reveille at 7:00 a.m., or stand quietly for "To the Colors" at flag raising every morning. There was "Retreat," just before supper when the flag came down, and of course "Taps," day is done, at lights-out time. I played many of the same tunes at meetings of my Boy Scout Troop 173.

At some point I found a second old bugle that was loose at the seams, and with the help of some Vaseline I rigged up a kind of slide bugle between the two. I could now get more than the four or five famous notes, and with the slide I started figuring out various tunes. One day I was working up *Orchi chornia* ("Dark Eyes"), one of my mother's favorites, when the doorbell to our fifth-floor apartment rang. I opened the door to be greeted by a tall, erect eighty-plus-year-old man with an impressive white walrus mustache. "I'm Nell Speck," he spoke, with a slight whistle. "I live on the sixth floor. I played cornet for John Philip Sousa. What kind of cornet are you playing?" I showed him my contraption and he said, "You need a real cornet." The very next day he brought one that he borrowed from a nearby fellow cornetist. I opened the case and my heart leaped. Valves! And all kinds of pipes winding about, and the smell of stale brass and moldy velvet. Nell Speck wrote out the fingering for the C scale and I was flying. Over the next few weeks he gave me lessons and told me stories of his playing days: how he supported his large family with two or three jobs a day—marches and picnics and party boats up the Hudson. And how he had fallen off his horse when he was playing for the inauguration of President McKinley! This last story works out date-wise; in March of 1897 Nell Speck would have been in his twenties.

Mother decided that I needed a "real" teacher. The daughter of one of my dad's fellow Baghdadians was taking piano lessons at a studio in Carnegie Hall. They had a trumpet teacher. We took the subway down to meet Jerome Cnudde.

Andrew Carnegie, famously, would not install elevators up to the balconies for the concert hall attendees, but for the apartments and studios on the 56th Street side of Carnegie Hall there was a magically silent hydraulic open-cage elevator that landed us on some upper floor. For the next four years, all through high school, I took that elevator to study with Mr. Cnudde. He told me he was French and Italian, which may have explained the elaborately curled blond mustache that he often trimmed during my lessons, when he wasn't drinking white wine or coffee. Mr. Cnudde must have been in his forties, a little too old for the on-going World War II draft. God love him, he was a jazz musician as well, and at the end of one of my first trumpet lessons he sat me down at the piano and showed me the blues chords in B-flat. Harmony lessons would soon follow. I learned to read music and could get around most of the difficult etudes in the Arban book, every beginning trumpet player's primer. Mr. Cnudde warned me off the newfangled bebop. "Listen to Louis Armstrong!"

Mr. Cnudde was one of two significant male teachers in my youth. The other was Rabbi Mosseson, who came to the house once a week to give me Hebrew lessons and help me prepare for my bar mitzvah. Rabbi Mosseson taught me more than Hebrew and Sabbath songs. He spoke about the mysteries of the universe, about possible connections between atoms revolving around a nucleus and planets around the sun.

My dad, who passed on a love of music, the Ur language of the soul, was conversely a man of few words. I have long searched for explanations, a way to excuse him for rarely fulfilling my lifelong need for a male mentor. In *Forty Days of Musa Dagh,* Franz Werfel creates a hero, a Levantine like my father, who climbs Mount Ararat, a holy shrine for Armenians, with the young son whom he loved. Yet he could not look upon his son's face, for to do so would be "looking into the face of God." Chaim Potok creates a Hassidic rabbi, Reb Saunders, in *The Chosen,* who brings his son up "in silence." Had Dad lived longer into my adulthood—he was only just beginning to soften from cutting me off after I married out of the faith—perhaps we would have bonded more. He had no difficulty interacting with his younger brother, Uncle Fahmi, who came to live with us when I was nine, a tall, dark, and handsome Adonis-like twenty-year-old, or being the life of the party when his Iraqi "boys" came around for Sunday *challys,* Arabic music, and food fests.

There was this man-man love—music, not sex, being the medium. The "boys" would arrive early Sunday afternoon bearing bottles of Metaxa brandy, strange vegetables (okra and eggplant), paper sacks carrying basmati rice, tiny bottles of rose water, *Amba* jars (later barrels) of mustard-cured mangos from India, and *Hail* (cardamon seeds). They took over the kitchen and started cooking. The *Towli* (backgammon) board would emerge and "Persian percussion," the staccato of the tiny dice and the slam of the wood-on-wood chips, commenced. Dad would start playing the old songs from Baghdad on his oud, his voice leading the others as they intoned the words of love and loss. Their inward-looking visages betrayed longing for the pace and light, the street cries and perfumes of the Babylonian city between the rivers. I was borne up by songs lauding *Aieeni,* her eyes, or dreams of romance, *yahabibi yaroochi,* a love life of glances and secret lust. It was my first connection to unrequited love that awaited me in a life unimaginable. At some point I would stand and sing *Yedi Sheddiyella-hahahaha,* trilling out the last grupetto like a muezzin calling the flock to prayer. These Jewish men were culturally Arabs and their essence was filtering into my soul.

Uncle Fahmi often played roughhouse with my brother and me, wrestling us both into submission. He taught us a hand-slapping game. We had to put out our hands palm down on one of his huge paws and try to dodge the incoming slap from the other. We played until our hands were red and swollen from being caught. It hurt so good! Fahmi, and my dad for that matter, led us in noisy games at the battle-scarred wooden, and mother-of-pearl inlaid, *Towli* board. We also learned to exhort, then fling, the tiny ivory dice and slap down the wooden checkers while calling out numbers in Turkish: *penj-yek*—five and one—or the coveted *du shesh*—double six! I loved and envied hearing Fahmi and my dad speak their mother tongue, Jewish (house) Arabic, to each other. And it pleased me when I caught on to their description of someone who was not quite right, as a *"shesh besh,"* one less than *du shesh,* double six, or missing a dot. Fahmi adored my dad. He listened to an old tape of Dad playing oud and singing until his dying day.

Dad and Fahmi always exuded a natural sense of belonging squarely on this earth, their being utterly comfortable as Jews, Arabs, Americans, no questions asked. Whereas Mother carried her ghetto heritage, always looking over her shoulder for the next pogrom, thankful she had escaped Christian vengeance. In light of what happened to her family, she was right to be afraid.

Coda

The message I got from Mom, and mostly ignored, was to keep a low profile about our religion (act British, think Yiddish). I am still discovering there has been all through my life a constant working out of my Jewish soul. I have loved and married and shared my beloved children with a woman who was from a nominal Christian background, as was Ellen Waldron, my remarkable second soul mate. Though I continue to fast on the Day of Atonement and lead a Passover seder (as more an homage to freedom for all mankind than a religious service), I do not believe in a biblical God. I do have a pantheistic respect for the Fates—where and when we are born determines so much. I stand in constant awe of the universe and our planet. I use the word *God* freely when conducting sacred works, imagining and respecting the mind-set of Verdi, Beethoven, Brahms, or Bernstein. And though there are those who say it is not reason enough, having been born in an era that witnessed the Holocaust, I call myself Jewish, often shout it to the heavens. I join Thomas Jefferson in mistrusting all preachers, and embrace American multiculturalism. One could argue that becoming an artist is a form of conversion. Music being in itself revelatory and spiritual is ergo a religion, a primal identity that trumps all others. Music is my faith.

I suppose that Leonard Bernstein and my psychiatrist Martin Bergman were my male mentor-models in later life—Jewish, but not "too," kind, strong, and knowing. Unsurprisingly, I find myself being mentor-model for many of my conducting students, a familiar comforting role; less so, for my own son, whom I adore—the face of God?

2

A Young Musician

♪

I developed my ear on the New York subways. The train ride between my high school, Brooklyn Tech, and Washington Heights took about forty minutes. I would choose a song that was popular, tune out the roar and clitter-clatter, and try to write out the notes and rhythms on a piece of music paper. When I got home I would test it on my trumpet. At some point I tried to write the names of the chords by ear and was able to test these when my folks got a piano for my brother. I taught my brother, Herbert, who was nine or ten at the time, to play chords from a "fake book," to hit the bass note with his left hand and then the three- or four-part chord with his right so he could accompany me, um-pa-um-pa, as I played my trumpet. Our big tunes were "Margie" and the "Sunny Side of the Street." This gave me the courage to start a band.

With a drummer and bass player/guitarist from Tech and an accordionist friend, I formed a dance band, the Stardusters. We played for teenage dances, always opening with the song our band was named after; I would stand tall behind my fold-up cardboard bandstand—we had three across, emblazoned with our name—and put my whole being into the song, vibrating on the long notes and thinking of the words as I played ...

> Sometimes I wonder why I spend
> The lonely nights—dreaming of a song

Our hero bands were Tommy Dorsey and Benny Goodman. And like thousands of bands before us we copied arrangements off of 78 recordings where we could, including Ellington and Juan Tizol's "Caravan," one of my solo specialties for which I had to learn to growl.

The Stardusters' audition for a hotel job in the Catskills, affectionately known as the Jewish Alps, was our demise. In the spring of 1949 we drove into the Manhattan theater district with all our band equipment to audition for a manager who placed bands in "Borscht Belt" hotels. Six or eight bands were clumped around a fairly large ballroom, clinging to their instruments until they were called upon to play the requisite swing tune, rhumba, or cha-cha-cha, and a *freilach,* a happy klezmer dance.

The manager had dismissed most of the bands but asked us to stay and we thought we had it made. But then came the difficult and rather cruel news. He liked the trumpet and the drummer, me and Bobby Rosen, but not the others. If we two wanted a job, he had a saxophonist and pianist he could team us with: "They cut a good show!" he reassured us. They were lurking in the corner, like scabs, and he called them out to meet us. They registered instantly as two squares: Paul Jacobs, a brilliant pianist from Juilliard who could read anything but did not have a jazz bone in his body (he needed sheet music for "Hatikvah" and the "Star Spangled Banner"!), and Martin Halpern, an Eastman Conservatory student who played a rather square clarinet (no Benny Goodman wannabe, he) and the alto sax.

I was spinning with disappointment, for my fellow band members and for musical reasons. These guys couldn't play jazz. And I disliked the alto in a small band. It mimics my trumpet range. I would prefer a tenor sax that can fill in the lower octaves with power and warmth. At stake were nine weeks of work, free room and board, and a thousand dollars minus 10 percent commission … my NYU tuition and more. Our two fellow Stardusters urged us to take the job and we did.

Our new mismatched band shared a big room with four beds and a bathroom at the Brookside Manor in the Catskills. Paul Jacobs was a Francophile. He played Debussy and read French classics all afternoon and went on to become a Pierre Boulez assistant in Paris. Paul and I actually had a fistfight over my coming in late "from being with your whore!" Bobby and I moved in with the casino gambling guy for the remainder of the summer. Twelve years later when I joined the New York Philharmonic, Paul was the orchestra pianist. Martin Halpern became an opera composer; I see him often at Queens College. Bobby Rosen took over his family painting contractor business in Brooklyn. Full disclosure: I was so shy in those days, my girlfriend and I hardly kissed.

As it turned out our square quartet played a mean *Rhapsody in Blue*. Marty and I covered the now iconic phrases for clarinet and wa-wa trumpet, Paul Jacobs played the hell out of the solo part and filled in the missing orchestra interludes. Years later it was Paul Jacobs's recording of the *Rhapsody in Blue* with the New

York Philharmonic, conducted by Zubin Mehta, that was used by Woody Allen in the opening of his film *Manhattan*. And yes, we could "cut" (sight read) a mean show.

On Saturday afternoons, usually still in our bathing suits, we rehearsed with the singers, dancers, and comedians for our big weekly show. That was our one look at the manuscript arrangements and "special material" until they returned for the show that evening. The entertainers spent all afternoon racing between hotels over narrow Catskill roads to rehearse their music—they tried to cover three hotels at a time—and they raced again that night all dolled up for the shows. I remember a particularly obscene act by Buddy Hackett, and an amazing triple-threat black singer, dancer, and trumpeter, Valaida Snow; I got to write a few arrangements for her after I complained her music was all marked up and unreadable.[1]

After the last show they gathered up their music, got out of their costumes, and headed back to New York, stopping off at the Red Apple Rest on Route 17, where a stream of Borscht Belt entertainers would share tales of the night's gigs: the close calls, the square or hip audiences, the terrific or not so terrific bands. I had a second Borscht Belt job at the Brookside Manor the following summer led by an older Yiddish theater violinist, Manny Fleishman, and his Radio Orchestra.

The Great American Songbook

All through my teens I was loading up on what we now call the Great American Songbook. I listened to big bands for half the night on my AM radio. It could reach stations halfway across the country after dark. I rarely missed "Your Hit Parade" on Saturday nights. I bought ten-inch records; "Green Eyes" was on the opposite side of "Amapola." I learned the newest show tunes from *Gypsy, Oklahoma,* and *Kiss Me, Kate,* within days of their opening. And I packed sandwiches and trained down to the Roxy or the Paramount Theater, timed so that I could catch two live shows, with singers and a big band, and a movie in between. At the nearby Uptown Theater, for ten cents, or nine cents and an empty Coke-a-Cola bottle, I saw Fred and Ginger, Nelson and Jeanette, Mickey and Judy, and thrilled to French horns leaping an octave in *Gone with the Wind.*

The music of one's youth sticks for life. I remember every tune and harmony I ever heard from my era, alas, not all the lyrics. And to this day I can sit at the piano and chord out hundreds of tunes in almost any key. This bedrock of pop tunes and the delicious harmonies of Kern, Gershwin, and Porter still lies beneath the several hundred symphonic works and operas I have studied and conducted starting in my twenties. It's my old testament.

Juilliard and NYU

I wanted to learn more about instruments and about arranging for more than four or five players, so after I graduated from Brooklyn Tech I enrolled in the Juilliard summer program. I was also accepted into the liberal arts program as a music major at NYU's Washington Square College and would attend in the coming fall.

Juilliard tested me in harmony and theory and although my ear was still in need of improvement, my eye was sharp, and

I got high grades. They registered me for classes in Beginning Piano, Orchestration with Adolph Schmid, and Conducting (they needed a trumpet player in the class). I got A's in the first two but failed conducting. Here's how that went. The class of about twenty musicians made up the orchestra. We studied Schubert's *Unfinished* and Beethoven's "Leonore Overture #2," works I had never heard—works I now know intimately.

I was a jazzman. I could play good Dixieland or a tricky *freilach,* or a reasonable facsimile of Billy Butterfield's "Stardust" solo. But I had played in the Brooklyn Tech Orchestra for only a short time, in particular for Mendelssohn's Violin Concerto. I could not yet transpose. And that trumpet part, simple as it was, was composed for a natural (keyless) trumpet "in E." I had to play an augmented fourth higher than what was written in my part—you look at a C but play an F-sharp above. Crazy! I was livid with not having the actual notes and penciled them into my part.

Back to Juilliard. We were in the middle of the Beethoven, and I was diligently counting measures when the music suddenly arrived at a long held note. All eyes turned toward me. "The call, the call," the students started whispering frantically. "What call?" said I. Every time I conduct Beethoven's "Leonore Overture #2"—I have since even conducted the entire opera *Fidelio*—and get to that magical moment of high drama when a far-off trumpet ("the call") announces the imminent arrival of the stage coach carrying the Minister, who will save the hero Florestan, I beam with laughter, thinking about my musical naïveté. Yet it seemed that no amount of embarrassment could dampen my passion for music, for something changed my life that summer.

The lucky among us remember the epiphanic moment we were converted, confirmed forever, to music. The novelist Ian McEwen describes it as "that sort of paradise-on-earth feeling of total absorption when time just falls away ... a complete evaporation of self awareness."[2]

We became alive with excitement and anticipation in the belief that yet another sublime musical experience awaits. To paraphrase Joseph Conrad, we become part of the timeless cycle linking humankind, "the past with the future, the living with the unborn." I believe that it is in pursuit of these sublime, ineffable moments that musicians are drawn to practice their art.

The former Juilliard building, now the Manhattan School of Music, was a confusing place. I got lost one morning, opened the wrong door, and walked into the middle of an ongoing rehearsal of the summer orchestra. Walter Handel was conducting, they were playing the wild "Dance Kastchai" from Stravinsky's *Firebird,* and the music entered my body, filling me with sounds I had never imagined possible. In the band were soon-to-be famous musicians whose names I later learned: Monday Ghittala on first trumpet, Johnny Swallow on trombone, Elaine Jones—a black *woman*—playing timpani! I vowed on the spot that I would learn more about this music and become a part of it.

The second epiphany came a year later. As luck would have it, Franz Bibo, a classmate at NYU, invited me to join the City Amateur Symphony. They rehearsed on Friday nights at the City Center on West 55th Street and were led by a redoubtable New York figure, a kindly municipal court judge, Leopold Prince. I arrived one Friday and sitting in the first trumpet chair was Monday

Ghittala, of Juilliard fame, who would soon join the Boston Symphony. On the podium was a guest maestro, clearly, even to my naïve understanding, a better conductor than old Judge Prince. I sat in the third trumpet chair, opened my music, and we began to play. The orchestra cellos opened with an arching leap and the woodwinds answered with odd but pleasing chords. The work slowly heated up and with Monday's help I was playing along until the waves of gathering sound overwhelmed me. I began to cry and left my chair to sit on the side and simply listen, to open my full being to the "Prelude and Love Death" from *Tristan und Isolde.* "That old poisoner" (*ce vieil empoisonneur*[3]), Wagner seduced me as he had so many others. I vowed to learn more about him and his haunting harmony.

The final epiphany, as if I needed another, came in summer of 1950. To earn extra money I was taking down (notating) songs for a very gifted songwriter, Ben Victor, who sang and played his music quite expertly at the piano, by ear—a time-honored gig plied by the young Gershwin for Irving Berlin, and unnamed others for Charlie Chaplin and Mel Brooks. Ben worked as a soda jerk at a drugstore on Broadway across from the soon-to-be-razed Brander Mathews Theater at Columbia University, and he gave me a ticket to an opera that was playing there starring Muriel Rahn and Lawrence Tibbett: *The Barrier,* by Jan Meyerowitz, a powerful story of miscegenation and patricide based on an early Langston Hughes poem, "Cross."

> My old man died in a fine big house.
> My ma died in a shack.

I wonder where I'm gonna die,
Being neither white nor black?[4]

I was writing a lot of music at the time, mostly arrangements; I had even orchestrated and conducted a full-length original musical by one of my classmates at NYU. But I left that theater vowing to become a serious composer, a composer of works like *The Barrier,* works that would change society. The senseless racism I witnessed during a trip to Florida in my early teens had never left me, and here was an interracial cast singing powerful music underscoring man's inhumanity to man. I had also witnessed my mother on one shocking Sunday afternoon learn the terrible truth that her six sisters and brothers, and her parents, had disappeared in what would soon be known as the Holocaust—we later learned they were taken to the Warsaw ghetto, never to be heard from again. (See photograph 5.) It was no surprise that I vowed my musical life must be committed to social change, to righting injustices. My liberal stance was in no way an intellectual decision—as a philosophy minor I was just starting to learn about David Hume and Karl Marx—it came from my early belief in the golden rule. I was simply an unsophisticated teenager searching for a better way. *The Barrier* was a defining moment for my music life yet to come.

"I'm moving out!" I was nineteen, living at home, and my parents and I, especially Mom, were fighting a lot. It was time. "I think that's a good idea," said Dad. This surprised and emboldened me. I quickly packed a small bag of clothes, toiletries, my trumpet, and music books and called Gabe Kosakof, a fellow NYU student who had connections at the Young Man's Hebrew Association, known now as the 92nd Street Y. He arranged to get me a room. It was a plan. I marched into the living room shaking and headed for the door, thinking, "Do I want them to stop me?" But Dad didn't even ask, "Where are you going? Do you have any money?" He simply said, "Call when you are settled."

The "Y" was a trip. I had a tiny dormitory room with a cot, a chest of metal drawers, and a small desk. There was a communal bathroom with showers. All this for nine dollars a week. I soon found a place to practice my trumpet down in the basement boiler room. Supper was often a can of sardines. Gabe got me a job as an usher for the Y's Kaufmann Auditorium, "New York's own Chautauqua," at a dollar an hour. There I experienced many concerts, dance events, and poetry readings, a rich cultural series produced by William Kolodney, education director of the Y. A spellbinding Truman Capote, dressed in a velvet Lord Fauntleroy suit and ascot tie, read *Other Voices, Other Rooms* with a high nasal twang. For Dylan Thomas I was sent to the local liquor store to buy a bottle of gin for his water pitcher.

My ushering job was at the height of the McCarthy witch-hunting days. Robert Frost felt obliged to begin his reading with a political comment, setting back the mostly liberal left New York audience, something along the lines of, "I am aware that many of you are unhappy with the current political climate but being from an old New England family, I find myself on the other side of the mountain." I refused to sign a YMHA loyalty oath, "For one dollar an hour?"

The Budapest String Quartet gave a Beethoven cycle. I searched for melodies á la Tchaikovsky. I was not yet ready for

the Viennese master's acerbic themes and their incredible unfolding. Eduard Steuermann played an all-Schoenberg piano recital.
I hated it! Dimitri Mitropoulos led a chamber music concert
featuring the back-chair members of the New York Philharmonic
that I was told he financed himself. I had recently attended his
rehearsal of the suite from Alban Berg's *Wozzeck,* one of the most
thorny and complex of scores, with the Philharmonic. And I sat
in awe when he corrected a wrong trombone note calling out
the bar number *from memory.* I found an excuse to get backstage
before the concert and there behind the curtain was my hero
Mitropoulos, an empty can in one hand, stooping down as he
picked up cigarette butts the musicians had thrown on the floor
in disregard of the warning sign and the provided can. There
was more: Mitch Miller's exquisite oboe solos at a concert of
Baroque music led by the millionaire cellist Daniel Saidenberg.
I remember concerts of African ceremonial dance by the Pearl
Primus Company. I watched the darkly handsome José Limón
dancing the title role in his *Moor's Pavane* to the music of Purcell's
Gordian Knot Untied, a seamless marriage of music and movement.
Little did I know that Limón and I would work together one day
as co-heads of a Bureau of Indian Affairs Pilot Project in support
of Native American culture (more later).

Martin Bernstein

Professor Martin (Luther) Bernstein, a charismatic self-taught musicologist at NYU, worked hard to supersede his Brooklyn-Jewish
roots. His passion for music not only matched my own, but was

backed up with what seemed like an infinite store of knowledge. I could hardly keep up. Martin Bernstein humanized the icons: J. S. Bach, labeling the opening measures of his orchestra pieces *"der hunds takt"* ("the dog's bar"), a mess so hopeless it was "thrown to the dogs" (I made my life's work conducting and I still think of the dog's bar story when I am about to give a first downbeat); Beethoven, deafened, scribbling in his conversation book about some lady he saw in the coffeehouse, "magnificent ass!"

Try as he would to poo-poo a career playing in an orchestra, Professor Bernstein could not avoid seeing music from the player's perspective. His description of the opening theme of the slow movement of Beethoven's First Symphony wasn't dryly theoretical, a "sequential passage outlining a triad," but psychoanalytic, a "highpoint in the life of the second violin player." I could see the second fiddles assuming their unusual task with care, imagine Beethoven chuckling to himself as he composed, "This will wake them up!" Decades before the arrival of "smart" classrooms, loaded with every Internet and media device, Professor Bernstein played taped recordings and showed slides of the exact passages in his orchestration class that demonstrated a composer's awareness of an instrument's timbre, or flexibility, or limitations: how Stravinsky avoided impossible slide shifts in the second trombone of *Firebird,* how Debussy fashioned seamless melody in *Afternoon of a Faun* by passing the melody imperceptibly from the flute to the oboe and back again. My lifelong curiosity and love of instruments began here.

He took great pride in my being chosen by another Bernstein as an assistant conductor of the New York Philharmonic, having once been a member of its bass section. And I kept up with Professor Bernstein. We talked about my first Beethoven Ninth, my first *Don Juan*. His wife, Dr. Virginia Lubkin, "Ginna," became our family's medical adviser. They were proud of their sons, a cellist and a harpsichordist, who played chamber music and went to Harvard to become doctors but ended up doing law. Oi! Harvard, the once forbidden fruit, that unattainable academic *shiksa* that bright Yiddish-speaking boys of Professor Bernstein's generation could only dream about. I was outraged when he was forced to retire by the very same Harvard men he gave jobs to. What Professor Bernstein possessed in one little finger ...

Yet he rarely showed disappointment or bitterness, at least to me. Our meetings continued to be filled with talk about music. I first learned from him about the number symbolism Bach built into his St. Matthew Passion when Jesus announces to his disciples, "One of you will betray me," and the response, "Lord, is it I?" appears in the chorus eleven times. And the twelfth response comes a few moments later when Judas alone asks, "Lord, is it I?" He remained my mentor, my professor, until I met another Bernstein.

Mannes School of Music

During my second year at NYU, I was invited to join the Mannes School orchestra as their first trumpet in return for lessons with Harry Freistadt, the principal trumpeter of the Columbia Broadcasting Orchestra. Under his tutelage I progressed rapidly. Within a year I played the difficult part in Stravinsky's *The Soldier's Tale* and was invited to play Haydn's Trumpet Concerto with the orchestra. Most of the faculty had escaped from war-torn Europe, and German was spoken as often as English. Many were former students of the Viennese theorist Heinrich Schenker, including our conductor, Karl Bamberger, a most passionate man who would one day become my conducting teacher. It was at Mannes that I made lifelong musical friends, among them Lamar Alsop, father of Marin, one of the first female conductors with a major career. Lamar was concertmaster for many of my later concerts and recordings.

Mills Music

In the fall of 1952, soon after I graduated from NYU, I searched the *New York Times* want ads for a job in music. Norman Warenbud, director of publications for Mills Music, was looking for an assistant. On the appointed day I put on my best suit and tie, took the subway downtown, and joined a long line of applicants on the second floor of the Brill Building, in the heart of the theater district. Built in 1931, the Brill Building was the slick art deco successor to the "jumble of brownstones known as Tin Pan Alley," where music publishers, song pluggers, writers, and arrangers kept offices. I got the job and joined Norman in a corner office on the second floor overlooking Broadway. Four stories above was the office of the arrangers, where I longed to be. On the ground floor at the lobby counter outside Lindy's Restaurant I had my morning coffee with a slab of their creamy cheesecake. Jack Dempsey's was a few doors north.

My job at Mills was about the printing and reprinting of sheet music, mostly pop songs and teaching manuals. I learned about music engraving and autography, the making of photo-ready masters for photo-offset printing, just as these hands-on methods, dating back to the sixteenth century, were becoming obsolete. My favorite task was going to the engraver with recent page proofs of sheet music in need of corrections. The engraver's workshop was in a rickety walkup a few blocks west in Chelsea. The air reeked of printer's ink that stained the thick wooden floors as well. I would show the engraver the page proof needing correction and he would fish through a stack of lead plates until he found the one that matched. Carefully laid-out ledger lines, clefs, and notes had been scratched and punched into the soft metal, mirror-image-backwards. He would find the corresponding lead plate, turn it face down on his work board, and with a broad hammer bang smooth the section that contained the wrong note or needed an accidental. He would then place it face up and I watched in awe as he plied his ancient craft, selecting from his rack a tool with which he rescratched the now-flattened ledger lines, and then pulling out the appropriate note head punch, opaque or hollow, he placed it squarely over the appropriate spot and gave it a solid whack. He then punched in a stem and flag as needed. The corrected plate was then brought to a proof press, an old screw down, not unlike those pictured in sixteenth-century paintings. It was laid on the bed, inked, and wiped, thus leaving the ink in all of the indentations. A clean sheet of paper was laid on top and the press was lowered and raised. Up came the crisp, slightly embossed corrected page proof for my inspection.

This careful, painstaking correction of a single note or addition of an accidental we can now do with a millisecond's stroke of a computer key. I wonder if looking every note and accidental *in the face* was reflected in the way musicians played as well, and whether the immense access and speed of our cyber world, whose brutal arrival I have witnessed, has dulled us. All I know is that to this day when I study a score I find my autographer-self lingering over the layout and note shapes, and I can easily separate computer-generated scores and parts from the earlier hand-engraved master editions of Breitkopf and Haertel.

My job at Mills Music required someone who was musically literate. But I soon realized very few people working nearby on the second floor could read their product, including my head boss and the leader of the firm, Irving Mills. I brought this up twenty years later with Duke Ellington. "Why does this guy Irving Mills have his name all over your music? I happen to know that he can't even read." Duke's response was unexpected: "Yes, his name is often down as composer or lyricist, but I sold him as many dogs as winners, and at the end of the week if I didn't have enough to pay the band he was there with a check."[5]

Thanks to Ellington, all the mortifying stories of Jewish or white exploitation of black artists took on another facet. Who was doing the hustling? Well before he hooked up with Joe Glazer, Louis Armstrong wrote about the wisdom of finding a smart "White Man" to act as a go-between, protecting him from being ripped off by club owners and record companies and letting him concentrate on making music.[6]

I never did make it up to the arranger's offices at Mills. But all through my college days I wrote arrangements: for Ben Victor's off-Broadway musical *The Merry-Go-Round* at the old Amato

Opera House on Bleecker street, soon to be home to Ted Mann's Circle on the Square; for the cabaret singers Valaida Snow and Thelma Pelish; for Ben Yost's male quartet, The Vikings, featured at Lou Walters's (father of Barbara) Latin Quarter. I was of course unaware when I handed out my band parts on the stage of the Latin Quarter nightclub that I was standing in very same space where twenty-five years earlier George Gershwin rehearsed his *Rhapsody in Blue* with Paul Whiteman's orchestra, and where Duke Ellington held forth when it became the downtown Cotton Club in the late 1930s. Gershwin, Whiteman, and Ellington would one day be central characters in my historic concert reconstructions and writings about American music.[7]

My greatest challenge was writing arrangements and orchestral accompaniments for an elegantly dressed quintet of lady harpists, Mike Lanin's Angelaires. It was easy enough to divide up their roles into bass line and rhythm, melody, and countermelody, but there are unusual limits to work around when writing for the harp. To begin with, harpists use only eight fingers, no pinkies. When we sit before a piano keyboard, all the notes, white or black, are immediately available—twelve notes to the octave. Not so the harpist who sits before an instrument strung with only seven notes to the octave, a do-re-mi scale (A–G); imagine the piano without black notes. Each of the seven notes can be made sharp or flat—throughout the harp, in every octave—by a foot pedal with three notches. When all the pedals are set in the middle (natural) notch, the harp plays a C scale. For the distinguishing glissando sweeps across the instrument, up or down, the pedals are set as close as possible to a chord. (For a C major glissando all pedals are in the middle notch, but we set the B pedal to B-sharp and the F pedal to F-flat, giving us extra *enharmonic* C's and E's.) Suffice it to say that arranging a piece of music that is chromatic, that changes key often, requires advanced planning. Debussy and Ravel often call for two harps to get around this problem.

The Angelaires appeared, among other places, with the Philadelphia Orchestra at the Robin Hood Dell, and in a hotel nightclub in Las Vegas. I received a postcard from one of the harpists describing their Vegas appearance. "We followed Roy Rogers and his horse Trigger, rolling out our harps with big smiles, dressed in our lovely matching gowns and white gloves, just as the sweepers finished clearing the stage."

Coda

As I gather together the shards of my peripatetic young music life, no recognizable form yet emerges. None of the above seems to point toward a career as a symphony conductor, or friendships with iconic figures. Talent and an abiding passion for music would open doors, and I would be welcomed by fellow believers. What is clear is that almost every time I moved out or on, good things happened. Perhaps I tend to see good in what happened, the better half of the partially filled glass?

3
On My Own

♪

In August 1953 I was drafted, kicking and screaming, into the US Army. I even spent a night in jail. And again my father set me straight. It turned out to be the best year and ten months of my young life, my private graduation into adulthood.

Most of my time in the army was spent as a member of the 173rd Negro Regimental Band at Fort Dix. Under President Truman's executive order the army began desegregation in 1951, two years before I was drafted. Korea loomed when I finished basic and band training. But I heard that the 173rd was looking for white musicians. I auditioned and was accepted. Besides playing for the usual parade gigs and regimental ceremonies, the 173rd had a big jazz band that rehearsed twice a week. This gave me an opportunity to write (and to hear!) dozens of my own arrangements and to mature as a writer and a trumpeter. In fall 1954 I was transferred to the First Army Band on Governors Island. All the barracks beds were taken so they made me a corporal and gave me "off post rations," meaning a supplemental raise in salary. I moved back with my old roommate, painter and bebop saxophonist Don Moffet, on West 15th Street, and took a ferry to work every day.

My army service was interrupted by an adventure, my first-ever trip to Europe and the Middle East, with a plan to visit my grandmother in Baghdad. Being stationed so close to New York, I had never used my furlough time and I was due about five weeks. My grandmother was still living in the family home in Baghdad. All my other grandparents had died without my ever knowing them and I often dreamed about seeing her. Momma Toba was legendary; married to a cousin at age thirteen, supposedly un-educated but foxlike clever, she had nine children and scores of grandchildren including me. The army had its own global airline, MATS (Military Air Transportation Service). With furlough papers in hand a uniformed soldier could hitch a ride through a program called Space Available Travel. I took a series of vaccination shots for Middle East diseases, got my first passport, and hitchhiked up to Westover Air Force Base in Massachusetts—hitchhiking in uniform was easy and safe at the time. Although many soldiers had been waiting for days for a space available flight, I lucked out. I was walking to the bathroom and a pilot shouted out to me, "What do you weigh, soldier?" "One hundred sixty pounds and I have a small duffel, sir." "Where are you heading?"

We took off an hour later for Scotland. It was my first plane ride. The plane had four propellers, the seats faced backwards, and the pilot was African American. Glasgow was cold but colorful. I recall orange tiled roofs and pink-kneed lasses in short tartan skirts. I stayed overnight and caught a plane to Paris, changed into "civvies" at the airport, and rode into Paris as just another American tourist. I found my way to Howard Brofsky and his wife, Mimi. They both had Fulbright fellowships. Howard was a former classmate working on his doctorate in the Italian Baroque and a terrific bebop trumpeter. They fed me and we caught up on NYU gossip. From Paris I was able to pick up MATS rides to Rome (there was only time for a pathetic plate of spaghetti at the airport), thence to Libya (my first artichoke—I tried to eat it with a knife and fork and chewed the leaves and the waiters stared in disbelief), and finally to Cairo, where I hoped to get a visa and a commercial flight to Baghdad. Instead I hit a stone wall.

I presented myself at the Iraq Consulate in uniform and filled out all the forms. What was the reason for my trip? "To visit my grandmother." Little did I know that our family name would be recognized as Jewish, and although I protested that I had been raised as a Methodist—that being the one church I played for the most—they would not give me a visa. Worse yet, they stamped my passport "Visa Applied For," a sign to other Arab embassies that I was an undesirable. I had a backup plan. I would fly to Beirut, where my father's sister, Aunt Salcha, and her four children lived. Her husband, Saleh Darwish, was in the import/export business. He would find a way to get me to Baghdad.

I decided to slow down and see the sights for a few days before approaching the Lebanese Consulate. Cairo was an amazing city. The drive in was through depressing slums but the city proper was alive with wall-to-wall people and cars. I remember beautiful houseboats along the Nile. I stayed at a first-class hotel; the bathtub seemed big enough to swim in. My few words of Arabic helped, but for one, *horrah*. It almost got me into trouble. I used it to express something bad or wrong, as had my dad and his friends; *horrah* turned out to be slang for poop. I did visit the pyramids and rode a camel. My candlelit dinner in a nearby hotel was elegant. The women, dressed in long, shiny gowns, were among the most beautiful I had ever seen, with dark, glowing skin and huge dark eyes. My Arabic roots were real. I felt curiously at home.

The young man at the Lebanese Consulate was about to give me a visa when he found the Iraqi stamp. "What happened?" he asked. I explained that I was trying to get to Baghdad to see my grandmother, and that I was a musician, and then came the white lie: "In the army, as you can see. I think they have a rule about entertainers, and they thought that I was Jewish but I was brought up Methodist." He was sympathetic, a lover of classical music, and an amateur pianist. He talked about working on a Beethoven sonata and I said that I had played trumpet for several of Beethoven's works in orchestras. As to the visa, the only way he could issue one was if I got a baptismal certificate from the Church of England! He would drive me during his lunch hour. I felt trepidation, to say the least.

He had a small MG. We rode through the English quarter with the top down and arrived at an imposing Anglican church. "Go to the office and ask for the priest. He will help you. I'll wait here." I told the priest my predicament. He smiled and started to fill out my baptismal certificate. "Aren't you going to ask me some questions?" I asked. Again that knowing smile and, "We do this all the time." I'm sure he knew what was going on, as did my new music-loving friend. When I got back to the car, he took the baptismal certificate and handed me my passport with the visa for Lebanon in place. I said that I might need the certificate, but he explained, "This is to protect me, not you."

Beirut was a gem. My tour guide was Uncle Saleh's jolly brother, Rachmin Darwish. I remember the Corniche running the length of the waterfront, lined with lovely restaurants and cafés. I was treated to a local delicacy indelicately named "lamb's balls." I was the lone visitor to a Roman ruin, the temple of Ba'al'bek, only a short car ride inland to the Beqaa Valley, tucked between two mountains. Someone bragged, "In Beirut you can ski the mountains and swim in the Mediterranean on the same day." Uncle Saleh was away in Paris; I would meet him on my way back. His eldest son, my cousin Akram, sweet and mild mannered, tried to approach the Iraqi Consulate on my behalf and failed. I later found out that by this time Grandmama Toba in Baghdad had learned about my trying to get through and was also trying to help. Cousins Simcha (Joy) and Joyce, who were in their late teens, spoke excellent French and English as well as Arabic. They read a lot and were delightful company. My aunt, who only spoke Arabic, was a love and couldn't do enough for me. Their home was very comfortable; beautiful Persian rug "paintings" were hung on the walls. I slept in a small bedroom with Akram. At the food market, Simcha and Joyce were not allowed to leave the car; they pointed to what they wanted to buy or described it and Akram made the purchase. That was when I realized they were strictly chaperoned and would be kept under wraps until they were married. I did not know at the time but even though I was a first cousin—we had the same grandparents for god's sake—I was a candidate.

It became clear that I would not get to Baghdad. So a marvelous farewell feast was laid out. It included a rare delicacy, unborn baby lamb, its pale almost white flesh plumped with rice and spices. It was delicious. As I write, I realize that MATS, the flying carpet provided by the US Army, did help me get a sense of Baghdad, and, through my darling Aunt Salcha, of Grandmama (Imi) Toba.

I quickly retraced my MATS route—Cairo, Libya, Rome—and arrived back at the Brofskys a world traveler. I had a week left on my furlough. Paris in January was very damp and chilly but it was Paris. I moved into a hotel near the Pantheon. I spent one day at the Besson trumpet factory and tried several new instruments before buying two to take home, for myself and for Roy Glover, a dear friend who was in the band on Governors Island. My life was about to change. Howard took me to Café Tournon, an American expat hangout. There I met two American girls, both named Gloria. I was drawn to the delightful young poet—Gloria Vando, smart, funny, and beautiful—who would one day become the mother of my three children.

A few weeks after I got back to New York I went out to my parents' beach home in Belle Harbor for supper and Dad suggested we take an after-dinner walk—the middle-class equivalent of brandy and cigars. He said that he had gotten a letter from his sister in Beirut, that they liked me very much and wanted to know if I would be interested in marrying Simcha!

"Dad, she's my first cousin!"

"We have had many first-cousin marriages in our family. [pause] They are offering seventy-five thousand dollars" (in today's dollars, half a million).

"Dad, she's my first cousin! And I'm not interested in getting married."

We walked on a bit and then he stopped, turned, and looked at me. "I think I can get you ninety!"

4
Seize the Day

♪

From this distance my dad's taking the arranged cousin-marriage offer seriously is sad as well as funny. I realize that my simplistic statement, "My parents made a new life in America," does not tell the whole story. They did prosper, placing them in a position to help many family members and bring up two boys, but their Old Worlds left deep shadows, conflicted hopes, perhaps passing regrets.

Cousin Simcha married another first cousin named Maurice. They have four excellent children and are very rich. So all's well on the Babylonian exile front. I opted for America.

Truth be told, I believed that marriage was a long way off when Dad and I took that walk. I always had a steady girlfriend, and I was staying in touch by mail with Gloria Vando. We had gotten quite close, hell, we were two young, attractive Americans in Paris! But marriage never entered my mind until she returned to New York in April. We started living together and then it became the natural next step. I was discharged from the army in June of 1955 and we "eloped" in July.

Carpe diem—it was time to seize the day! I wanted our marriage to be a time of joy, not a referendum on intermarriage ... is there any other kind? Naïve perhaps, even selfish, where my parents were concerned, but the alternative was too painful to imagine.

We honeymooned on Avenue A in an artist's loft and soon left in our Ford two-seater, "Willy Shakes," for the Shakespeare Festival at Antioch College, in Yellow Springs, Ohio. I played in the band and composed incidental music for *All's Well That Ends Well*. On the way back to New York we visited the Canadian Shakespeare Festival.

I lucked out and found an apartment, a "cold-water" railroad flat up five unforgiving flights on the corner of Sullivan and West 4th street: tub and sink in the kitchen, toilet off the long narrow hall, $24.00 a month. The all-purpose front room faced north and we could see the Empire State Building from our window, the same window through which an old upright was hauled up on ropes and stationed in the kitchen next to a big brick wall filled with old covered-over flue holes; it was very *La Bohème*.

Two years later my mom climbed the five flights with gifts and a feather pillow to see her new grandchild, Lorca Miriam Peress, born January 2, 1958. Dad stayed away, still disapproving of my marriage out of the faith, but after he died we found a certificate in his safe deposit box from the Radio City Synagogue; he arranged to have Lorca's name blessed before the Torah the week of her birth.

I returned to the Mannes Orchestra as their first trumpet, and eventually became assistant conductor under Karl Bamberger. I also returned to my MA studies in Musicology at NYU and by 1958 I was teaching sight singing and was asked to take over the Washington Square Chorus and Orchestra. I was conducting every week now, planning programs and learning new scores.

Mannes and NYU gave me a sort of old world stability, but there was another nonacademic music life beckoning—more dangerous, more creative, one that served the living and emerging arts. A want ad appeared in the *Village Voice,* looking for a "composer to write incidental music for Shakespeare." I called and spoke with the director, Joe Papp, about my *All's Well That Ends Well* score. Papp told me he had just hired someone. A prophetic moment; my life (and David Amram's life) might have been very different if I had called earlier.

A few weeks passed. I was on the union floor of Local 802, hanging out in the trumpeter's corner at the Thursday morning shape-up, hoping to get a Saturday night dance gig, when three of us were hired for a recording session: incidental music for a new Shakespeare Festival series (oops) being held in a church in Greenwich Village, directed and produced by Joseph Papp, then an unknown. The composer and conductor was another unknown, David Amram.

David Amram

The music for *Titus Andronicus* was recorded in some office space near 23rd Street and Broadway. I sat myself down in the second trumpet chair. David, being David, had written a tricky little solo in my part and I tossed it off. He whipped around as I finished.

"Who are you?" he asked. "Maurice," said I. "*Mon*reece!" said he, the first syllable rising in surprise as if he were introducing me to his audience … my mon Reece. I would eventually call him Am-stein, to somehow proclaim his Jewish roots aloud, to spite the patrician face and prep school manner.

From that moment on I became his solo trumpet player, and eventually his contractor (I would help hire the players and see that they got paid) and a close lifelong friend. This was the first of what would be many Papp Shakespeare productions with music by David that firmly established the New York Shakespeare Festival in Central Park.

We mostly recorded in a studio in the West 40s, and I would stay on well into the wee hours, while David did a final "mix." The sessions were done on reel-to-reel tape, and edits were made with scissors and Scotch tape. After one of these all-night sessions we walked together down a deserted Fifth Avenue to our homes in the Village, and in that special quiet of a big city near dawn, high on life and music, we shared our dreams, mine to conduct, his to write concert music. He was working on a string quartet, he shyly admitted.

NYU sorely needed some community outreach and in 1959 the administration asked me to put together a series of free outdoor public summer concerts in Washington Square. So I suggested to David that he add a bass part to one of the movements of his string quartet to make it more orchestral, and I would include it on a program that summer. As luck would have it, it rained the day of the concert and we moved indoors for the world premiere of *Autobiography for Strings*. David dedicated it to our newborn, Lorca.

I started conducting for David: a "Sacred Service" at the Park Avenue Synagogue, commissioned and movingly sung by Cantor David Putterman; a recording of his spiky *Shakespearian Concerto*; and eventually a full evening of his music at Town Hall. I remember Am-stein, during the dress rehearsal, as he practiced running down the aisle seeing if he could leap upon the stage to accept the forthcoming crowd's applause. And yes, a crowd of beatniks and village people, hippies and local storekeepers, charmed by the force of his belief in himself and his lingo, a stream of folksy truths and unmaskings of everything and everybody beginning with himself, did in fact turn out. If you were to hear David sing the talking blues to his own slashing guitar licks, diving into the next verse without knowing how he will make the rhyme, or the idea come out—a virtuoso tidal wave of social commentary, witticisms, and doggerel—you would know what a daring jazz genius he is. We were all of us, from Joe Papp to the local news guy, entranced.

David composed the score for the now classic film *Splendor in the Grass*. It opens with a long bluesy unaccompanied trumpet solo—my proudest playing on record—as we watch the young, beautiful star-crossed couple, Natalie Wood and Warren Beatty, making love in the grass. "Gadge," Elia Kazan, staged a huge, wild, and drunken dance hall scene with dozens of extras that we filmed one morning in the gym of a private school in Riverdale; there are glimpses of me playing live in the Dixieland band. I was also the contractor of the musicians, and after the lunch break I sought out Kazan to find out what next. He was in a quiet huddle with Natalie Wood. It was a diva moment. Her curl had turned differently from the morning and she would not allow the on-site costume and wig people to touch it. We all waited for an hour until her hairdresser drove up from Manhattan and got her squared away. Being the clock-watcher on the job I was impressed with Kazan's patience and appearance of total sympathy as the dollars ran up.

I introduced David to Bernstein and he was soon appointed as Composer in Residence to the New York Philharmonic; I took him to Otto Perl's, my tailor (and Bernstein's), to fit him up for a set of tails; and I eventually handed the baton to him in Corpus. He was a natural! Only a few years ago, in 2009, there was an early morning emergency call from Russia: "Monreece, help! I'm conducting Bloch's *Schelomo*; do you conduct that section where the band is in six and four at the same time ... ?"

David is ever a positive force, unflappable in contretemps: with Putterman, with high strung and "high" players, and with deadlines. In the early folk-song and Beatle days I complained, lamented, to David that I had read that more guitars were sold that year than Bibles and the kids were only playing three chords. "That's okay, Monreece, they touch music, next thing you know, they will explore jazz, the blues, Segovia!"

I recently brought my orchestra to Symphony Space to celebrate what Amram titled "The First 80 Years." There was a sold-out packed audience—patricians, old and young hippies, yarmulkes, and kids, just like in Town Hall forty years before. I invited David to be the composer-in-residence at a Conductors Workshop I was running at Queens College, and we studied and played one of his Native American inspired works, *Kokopelli: A Symphony in Three Movements*. The transcription he does of a traditional love-flute melody is meticulous, filled with tiny but necessary details, ghost notes, bends, quick turns. In the piece he has the whole orchestra play the melody, inviting in one section at a time to live in its space before the variations begin, gaining respect for the rich inordinate nuance within what sounds so simple and natural.

David is a modern Pied Piper, literally, on sundry pipes and whistles—Native American love flutes and Irish penny whistles, an Arabic shenai—that he carries around with him, scrambled together in a bag. Some hang around his neck on his ever-growing trophy-necklace of medals, crosses and stars of David, magic feathers, and similar talismans gathered on his travels. And David is a Pied Piper in spirit, one who draws people from every walk of life to follow his passions for music of every stripe and for brotherhood and peace on earth. Some see this as an act, but David is the same David be it before a public audience or one on one.

Coda

Dianu, "enough," we sing at the Passover seder just before the meal is served; enough was done to save our people, we dare not ask for more. *Dianu,* I was conducting at NYU, and *dianu,* I was conducting at Mannes, and *dianu,* for my gigs with David. But only a few months after we set up house in Greenwich Village, I added to the mix a brass quintet, the Chamber Brass Players, and we garnered attention for an unusual concert series.[1]

Following a sixteenth-century German tradition, we played "tower sonatas" and chorales from the belfry of Stanford White's Judson Memorial Church that still looms above Washington

Square Park. The park was the gathering place for the first wave of guitar-strumming folk musicians, and where many hopeful local artists displayed their work at the annual springtime Washington Square Outdoor Art Exhibit. Somehow I gained permission for our Chamber Brass Players to haul ourselves, our music stands, and our instruments up a ladder and through a trapdoor in the middle of a girls' dormitory room, and onto the windy, bird-dropping-filled, open balcony of the church where we faced uptown and started our tower music concert with *Pictures at an Exposition.* The very classy *New York Times* and the *Village Voice* sent photographers who climbed up the ladder for a most dramatic shot of us blowing our brains out. It took in the rooftops north of the park below and made the front page. (See photograph 6.)

One of my savvy musical buddies, the violinist Ray Kunicki, presciently told me I had broken through. I was unwittingly getting a crash course in concert giving; I had to raise money from local storekeepers to match the Union Trust Fund so we could get paid. I prepared programs with original artwork by my old roommate Donald Moffett and had them printed. I wangled new works from my composer buddies, David Amram among them, and kept the band sharp. Ray was right—soon came a recording contract and other gigs.

After our second season of tower concerts the pastor of the Judson Church, in charge of community outreach, invited my young family—Gloria Vando Peress, now an NYU student, budding poet, and young mother of Lorca, age two—to move a block away, from our five-story walkup on Sullivan Street to a charming basement apartment in the church's annex on Thompson

Street: fifty-five dollars a month. The apartment included a small backyard for little Lorca, and shortly her brother Paul, and there were dozens of college-age babysitters in the adjoining student residence. We were witnesses to the first-ever "happening," sponsored by the church—a topless, ash-covered, groaning woman in a room filled with Claes Oldenburg constructions depicting an atomic holocaust. We had Langston Hughes, Jan Meyerowitz, and the cast to dinner there when I was preparing their powerful opera *The Barrier,* the opera that so deeply moved me ten years earlier. *The Barrier* was the most ambitious event of what would be my third and last free summer concert series sponsored by NYU. And by this time we were performing indoors in their new Eisner-Lubin Auditorium. The first two summers we did new works by Robert Kurka, David Amram, Gunther Schuller ("Transformation" with the Bill Evans Trio), and Sam Barber's "Knoxville" with the young soprano Martina Arroyo. There were symphonies by Mozart and Haydn, and an all-Bach concert.

Six Words

Ray Kunicki, my oracle, was playing principal second violin in the summer orchestra. He gave me an invaluable music lesson at an early rehearsal. I call it "Six Words." I must have been talking too much trying to describe some nuance and probably losing the band when Ray came to my rescue: "Mo! Six words—fast/ slow, short/long, loud/soft—that's all we need." He was telling me to keep the poetry and narratives to myself and use the time to let the musicians learn the music. The Six Words, in phonetic translations, to which I add the cardinal numbers, "good morn-ing," "good afternoon," and "thank you," have served me over the years on crib sheets I made up for rehearsals in China, Korea, Czechoslovakia, Italy, France, and Germany.

Gordon Davidson

Just around this time Dave Amram wrote the score for Norman Corwin's *The Rivalry,* a Broadway play about the Lincoln-Douglas debates with Dick Boone, Martin Gable, and Nancy Kelly. I was the cornet player in a five-piece band that appeared onstage, dressed in Civil War costumes. We played David's period-sounding *entr'acts* for the several scene changes. One of *The Rivalry*'s ASMs (assistant stage managers) was the charming, beguilingly dimpled, well-grounded Gordon Davidson. We became good friends, and when the time came for the third season of the NYU Summer Concert Series I asked him if he would help me with the climactic scene of *The Barrier.*

In the opera, Cora stands over the body of her "husband" after having sent her patricide son to hide, and sings a bitter aria of loss and fear and grief, ending with, "Damn you, Colonel Tom. Damn you, Thomas Norwood. Go-d ... [slur to high C sustained!! Then down to a shouted] ... *Damn you!*" We were doing a concert ver-sion but I felt that this extraordinarily powerful moment should be staged and I gave Gordon a copy of the vocal score. He came back the next day with the Langston Hughes poem (quoted earlier) and the subsequent play *The Mullato* before it was turned into an opera libretto for *The Barrier.*

With Meyerowitz's help we assembled a fine cast. Rawn Spearman played the son, and Gwendolyn Walter—a recent winner of the Marian Anderson Award—sang the role of the mother. Minor roles were played by the young Nico Castel and Richard Bernstein; both went on to work in the Met. When Gordon finished staging the "Damn you, Colonel Tom" scene, the cast sat stunned. They talked among themselves and asked for a conference with me and Gordy. "If you will stage the entire show, we will throw away our vocal scores and memorize everything."

It was Mickey and Judy instant theater, but *in fact*—not on film. So what if we had set aside only a single week of rehearsals? In the remaining time Gordon staged the entire opera rather brilliantly and got a young architect/designer, Peter Wexler, on board to create a stage set and lighting. We had to scrounge up a jukebox, a spotlight, a few lighting "instruments," poles to hang them on, and a small light-board brilliantly run by a music student, Paul Fran. The small but potent orchestra was now set up beneath the stage as in a pit. The NYU porters at the time were all men of color. They knew the significance of what we were doing and bent all the rules to help. Thanks to Judy Davidson, who was working for a Broadway press agent, our performance drew critics and we got excellent reviews in all the major papers. The university provost called to ask if it was possible, and how much it would cost to do another weekend and invited me to lunch at a classy French restaurant with a Miss (Alice) Tully, an opera supporter. I was in a fog—which fork do I use? Is this *my* glass? She sang what she described as "The Vintner's Song" to the sommelier and talked about a trip around the world she was about to take, visiting geysers, and timed so that she arrived just as they were about to erupt. Not a word about *The Barrier.* When we left, the provost said, "We have the money." And so *The Barrier,* my swan song to NYU, lived on a bit longer.

The powers that be at NYU began to court me after the success of *The Barrier* and the New York Philharmonic appointment. We were offered a lovely faculty apartment on Eighth Street off of Fifth Avenue—two bedrooms and a full kitchen with a pass-through window into a living room that looked onto Washington Mews. Raymond Ericson's highly complimentary review in the *New York Times* (July 27, 1961) closed with a reference to my becoming "one of the three assistant conductors with the New York Philharmonic next season. And this foretaste of his ability suggested how well he deserved the honor."

5
The New York Philharmonic

♪

hen Leonard Bernstein was appointed music director of the New York Philharmonic in 1958, he instituted a novel assistant conductors' program, ostensibly to develop American talent. One of the first to be chosen was my upstairs neighbor on Sullivan Street and musical colleague at the Mannes School of Music, Stephan Bauer Mengelberg, nephew of the famous Dutch conductor. What seemed a world away suddenly came within reach and I, too, applied. In February of 1961, a letter arrived from the Koussevitsky Foundation inviting me to meet Mr. Bernstein at a gathering to be held in his studio apartment at the Osborne, Stanford White's massive brownstone-and-stained-glass edifice diagonally across the street from Carnegie Hall. I thought I was crossing the Rubicon when I entered the lobby on a Friday afternoon, March 10, 1961. I decided not to cancel a pair of Young Audience concerts with the Chamber Brass Players I was to play earlier that day, thinking I would be less nervous than if I just waited about. The five of us were crammed into a small sedan, with the tuba as a sixth passenger. By the time I struggled out of the car when it dropped me off on 57th Street, my Irish tweed suit and hand-loomed wool tie were a rumpled mess. Under my arm, in the hip fashion of the day, I carried my green corduroy trumpet bag.

The Osborne was intimidating, a long canopy, liveried door-men, birdcage elevators. "Yes, Mr. Bernstein is in studio 2DD on the second floor." I entered the studio to find five or six other men in their twenties seated about, not knowing whether to talk or study the ceiling. I was glad I had my horn with me. Its familiar tubes and twists under the corduroy kept my hands occupied. Bernstein arrived, cigarette in hand. He explained that according to our resumes, all of us were qualified to be assistant conduc-tors with the Philharmonic; therefore he was following the lead of Harvard's medical school. When faced with more deserving applicants than they had room for, the medical school faculty came up with the novel idea of holding cocktail parties where they would meet and observe the candidates in a social setting to help them decide whom to accept.

To start things off Bernstein asked each of us why he wanted to become a conductor. One frustrated fellow immediately ques-tioned the entire proceeding, demanding that Lenny sit at the piano so that he could demonstrate his conducting prowess. An-other told of playing viola in several orchestras, that he found most conductors to be charlatans (oops). "It was time that a player from the ranks, one with orchestral experience, be noticed," he said.

When my turn came, I told Bernstein the truth: That I had been curious and passionate about music ever since I was a little boy and my dad sang and played Arabic folk songs for me on his oud—that got him! That when I was a Boy Scout I used to fit two bugles together, making a kind of sliding trumpet, so I could get the "in-between notes." That even though I was now playing the trumpet professionally, teaching theory, writing arrangements, and conducting whenever the opportunity arose, it was only when I was leading an orchestra that all of my musical interests came together and I was totally focused, without nervousness, fully occupied with the music. When the gathering ended, I was the first to leave. In my heart I felt that I would be chosen.

A few days later Miss Helen Coates, who introduced herself as Mr. Bernstein's personal secretary, called to tell me that I had been chosen to be one of his assistants. She said that I would receive a confirmation in the mail: "But say nothing to anyone about this except to your family, until the official announcement appears in the newspapers." A month passed before the announcement appeared in the New York *Herald Tribune* on April 12, 1961. The heading read "3 Assistant Conductors Named by Philharmonic for 1961–1962," and below were postage stamp–sized photos and the simple caption, "John Canarina and Maurice Peress, two New Yorkers, and Seiji Ozawa, of Japan." (See photograph 7.)

The family deserved a vacation, a brief stay before the Philharmonic season started. On the beach in Shelter Island I met the composer Earl Robinson. We were introduced by the actor, and onetime folk musician, Alan Arkin. Earl had a kindly face, unblinking attentive eyes, coupled with unguarded access to his core beliefs, beliefs I could share. We spoke for an hour or more about his powerful music theater piece, *Sandhog*, another social activist opera I had seen and was impressed by, and my recent success with *The Barrier*. I told him about my pending stint with

Bernstein and the New York Philharmonic; he told me about his most recent work, a concerto for the singing banjo player Pete Seeger—premiered by Fiedler and the Boston Pops—and how Eric Weissberg joined to cover much of the virtuoso solo banjo parts. Fellow travelers, in more ways than one, we had much to share. Earl was one of those precious few truth talkers who become instant, lifelong friends and confessors.

Bernstein and the New York Philharmonic

During the Philharmonic's short preseason southern tour in September 1961 it became abundantly clear that life around Bernstein would never be dull. In Baltimore there were two civil rights protests on the same day. I proudly followed as Bernstein led me and several members of the orchestra out of a famed seafood restaurant that refused to seat us because Sanford Allen, a black man, was in our party. But that very same night Bernstein had the orchestra play "Dixie" as an encore, catering to the lingering Confederate past. "They like it!" he said. The Philharmonic percussionist, Arnie Lang, a drummer friend from my dance band days, who was supposed to play cymbals on "Look away! Look away! Look away, Dixieland!" stomped off the stage.

Two other young conductors shared my tenure as assistant conductors with the New York Philharmonic: the solid and steady Juilliard graduate, John Canarina, who charmed everyone with his droll sense of humor and impressed even Bernstein with his encyclopedic knowledge of repertoire and conductors; and Seiji Ozawa, a doll-like, young and brilliant talent from Japan who had studied with Von Karajan and captivated everyone. We three assistants were previously unknown to one another; we met at the first rehearsal.

John had studied with the legendary Pierre Monteux and led the Seventh Army Symphony. A half century later John would author books about both: *Uncle Sam's Orchestra* and *Pierre Monteux, Maitre,* a fine biography. His third book, *The New York Philharmonic: From Bernstein to Maazel,* appropriately frames the musical generation that John, Seiji, and I shared. Seiji had made a huge impression on Bernstein at Tanglewood, where he would one day reign as music director of the Boston Symphony Orchestra and where a new hall would be built in his name.

We met with Bernstein to discuss how we would divide up the season. He said rather than being responsible for entire concerts we should divide the works for each concert between us, and rotate between the bigger symphonies and concertos and smaller works as we saw fit.

Assistant conductors are expected to take over a concert or a rehearsal at a moment's notice. I was called twelve hours before the first rehearsal of Roy Harris's Seventh Symphony and told Mr. Bernstein was indisposed. I stayed up all night studying, and the next morning I rehearsed a work I had never heard (except in my mind's ear), or conducted, and the band had never played. Another time the three of us were told that Bernstein was too ill to conduct and we would be conducting at a special concert being given in White Plains. We were driven by limousine to John's home in nearby Tuckahoe where we dressed and had a final look at our scores. I was covering the "Three Cornered Hat" of Falla. I remember the three of us in our new tails, each in a different room, singing and conducting away for the big night. The limo brought us to the hall. The players were warming up. We stood with our scores and batons at the side of the stage ready to go on when Bernstein showed up. "I feel better. Let me do the Beethoven; we'll see if I can continue." Of course he conducted the entire concert. Euphoria, cheek to jowl with disappointment, marks every artist's life. But we were angry for the first and only time that year.

I cannot complain; Bernstein was generous. We each had a debut piece with the orchestra and appeared on a Young People's Concert that was televised. Only recently I visited the Philharmonic Archives with a class of young conductors to show them scores that had been used and marked by Mahler, Toscanini, and Bernstein. Barbara Haws, the curator, surprised me when she began the visit with a fifty-year-old videoscope of a young conductor, me, accompanying bassist Gary Karr. I had never seen myself on TV during my Philharmonic year—there were no rebroadcasts in 1962—and there I was … in my morning suit, striped pants, ascot tie, and spats … not embarrassing myself. My official debut on a subscription concert was with Eric Satie's tongue-in-cheek *Parade*—a Picasso, Cocteau, Diaghilev ballet score, punctuated with ragtime, pistol shots, ratcheting roulette wheels, and a clattering typewriter with a bell. "Just stand there and let it happen," said Lenny. You bet.

I made the youthful mistake of rushing to turn around for a bow the moment I heard the applause at the end. Helen Coates was waiting for me offstage. "Young man, *never* take a bow while your orchestra is seated." I was certainly excited; my Baghdadian family had come to the concert. It would be their first visit to

Carnegie Hall and for some their first concert ever. I spotted my Grandmama Toba, who had just arrived from Baghdad. What did she think about this affair, the rituals, the strange music, me up there onstage? I saw Uncle Eddie walking up and down the aisle, never sitting. After the concert some of my family came backstage. My dad walked straight up to the pianist Robert Casadesus, who had just played the Saint-Saens fourth concerto, to say, "God bless your hands!"

Seiji and I also performed, and later recorded, Charles Ives's "Central Park in the Dark," an unusual work from ca. 1901 that tells the story of a dramatic event in Central Park—Ives lived alongside the Park on West 65th Street—and requires two conductors. The string orchestra was conducted by Seiji; it sets the quiet evening atmosphere of the Park with slow-moving, mildly dissonant chords—a ten-measure phrase that is constantly repeated. I led the second orchestra, a few winds and brass, drums, and two pianos. After the strings settle in we hear snatches of a waltz tune in the clarinet, and a flute and oboe hint at other melodies as if from a distant band, and at faster tempos. A piano plays a fragment of a ragtime lick. (Ives played and sang in the Banjo Society at Yale, and they featured the newly popular ragtime tunes.) More instruments enter and at last we make out a peppy ragtime tune from one of the pianos, "Hello Ma Baby," written in 1899 by Joseph E. Howard and Ida Emerson, the first song recognizing the telephone:

> Hello! ma baby,
> Hello! ma honey,
> Hello! ma ragtime gal!

Send me a kiss by wire,
Baby, ma heart's on fire!
If you refuse me,
Honey, you'll lose me,
Then you'll be left alone,
Oh, baby, telephone,
And tell me I'm your own!

Other instruments enter with the "Hello, ma baby" tune in canon—a trumpet, a trombone, a high-pitched E-flat clarinet—ever gaining in speed and volume. You can see that I was having all the fun. I cue a third group, they enter at an even faster clip, a brisk 6/8 marching cadence led by a second thumping piano, a snare drum, and piccolo; they depict a runaway horse galloping toward the bandstand. The music gets wilder and ... CRASH! The ragtime and marching bands stop dead, revealing the quiet calm of the strings, the dark, always present atmosphere of the park. A pair of solo violins sighs and the repeated phrase in the strings fades away. Ives was curious about simultaneity, what happens when two or more pieces of music, going at different speeds, pass by one another. "Central Park in the Dark" opened me to sound as sculpture, another way of listening, and prepared me for Ives's disciples, John Cage, George Antheil, and my friend Morty Feldman.

Life with the NY Phil'

My Philharmonic year was the orchestra's seventieth and, alas, its final season in Carnegie Hall. As we would discover, Carnegie Hall's legendary acoustics and history were irreplaceable. The hall itself was slated for demolition; so much for my fantasy that all of the historic performances, back to Tchaikovsky's opening concert in 1891, had somehow implanted themselves, left a nano-sonic imprint, somewhere on the walls and ceiling of the hall that we would one day be able to recover. Backstage facilities were primitive and overtaxed. Each of the players had a small gym locker sufficient for their concert clothes. Most carried their instruments to and from home. We three assistants had no locker so we flitted happily from the stage wings to Maestro's dressing rooms with our scores in hand. When the season ended and the men were cleaning out their lockers, Louis Ricci, a longtime horn player in the orchestra, found two Toscanini batons he had kept as souvenirs and thought I should have them. Among the musicians, and especially among the Italian musicians who played under Toscanini, *Il Maestro* was a god. I was honored of course and have kept them ever since.

I learned so much from the players. Sol Goodman, long-reigning timpanist during the regimes of Toscanini, Fritz Reiner, Dimitri Mitropoulos, and Bernstein used to call me over to explain some subtlety of his art; assistant conductors were there, after all, to learn. He showed me how, for example, he played the "heartbeat" at the end of the first movement of Tchaikovsky's *Pathetique* with one stick, because it was easier to match the exact weight of each stroke; meanwhile, with his other hand, he could dampen the sound, producing just the length necessary. He demonstrated how he used a bare, unpadded, wooden stick for the second timpani entrance in Strauss's *Don Juan,* producing a "drummier," more explosive sound. But my most memorable lesson was the day he made me aware of how indeterminate the downbeat can be.

Goodman explained that when he approached a big opening chord for the full orchestra, like the one that clears the air for the *"Eroica"* Symphony, or the third "Leonora Overture," he would wait for a microsecond, after everyone else in the orchestra started their entrance; wait, while the sounds collected; and with his timpani stroke, itself a form of gathering force, he would establish the actual perceived center of the beat, a humbling thought for a novice conductor practicing his own downbeat.

Another example of the flexibility and indeterminacy of time was suggested by a remark made to me by Harold Gomberg, the solo oboist in the New York Philharmonic, known for his ravishing, time-stands-still playing. Gomberg told me that he never counted *"one,* two, three; *one,* two, three," in three/four time, but *"one, one, one, one, one, one,"* to avoid giving the downbeats importance. Like all great artists, Gomberg analyzed the phrases within and over the measure lines as he played, flowing toward and resting on important notes, adding a more or less luscious or impersonal sound and more or less vibrato. Composers since Bach have exploited the oboe's extraordinary expressive powers and assigned the most important vocal-like lines to them. Along with the concertmaster, who guides the first violin section in a similar fashion, a principal oboist sets the musical standards for the whole orchestra.

The legendary Mademoiselle Nadia Boulanger, whose composition students included Aaron Copland and Virgil Thomson, was a guest conductor that year. Thanks to my fractured French, I was assigned to escort her to rehearsals, and more than once in the backseat of the limousine she spoke to me of the "tyranny of the bar line," its artificial magnetism, the need to "bounce off" quickly.

I have since taken the notion of flexible time even further, what I call my additive, or Zen, approach. Rather than thinking of music as being hitched to a metronome, the notes following each other mathematically or mechanically, I imagine a musical phrase as the sum of individual notes examined and sounded one at a time. It is not unlike stringing a necklace from a pile of precious beads; a long fat bead (a long quarter note) is threaded and then knotted in place, then a slightly shorter skinny bead (a short quarter note) is threaded and its knot is tied. Others follow, slightly longer and shorter, fat ones and skinny ones. The necklace—the phrase of music—will not bunch up but rather have a relaxed shape if each bead, or note, is given proper space before the knots are tied, before the beat (or the bar line) intrudes. For example: "L o n g, short, **fat**, skinny" is one way to sing the four equal notes in "Come to me my (Melancholy Baby)." Or, "skinny, l o n g, short, **fat**" is one way to sing the four equal notes "I loves you Por-(gy)." Words, not four metronomic notes, shape the phrase; and so it is in instrumental music, when performed—dare I say sung—by a player or led by a conductor who is sensitive to the tensions and relaxations of harmony and melody; the notes are again slightly longer or shorter, and fat or skinny, in order to produce a fully formed phrase. Singing has always been the sine qua non for instrumental music. Wagner attacks "four-legged Kappelmeisters," who beat time "like turning out so many sausages."

During concerts, Seiji, John, and I usually sat in or near Maestro Bernstein's box and we took pride in gaining an extra bow for Maestro and favored soloists by becoming a claque. If the applause seemed in danger of dying down before the desired effect, we turned on a flurry of random applause until others in the audience joined. We rarely failed.

One of our favorites was the Viennese maestro Josef Krips, whose baton style could most kindly be described as awkward, yet he achieved with his eyes and his iron will the most sublime performances of works by Beethoven and Mozart. For what seemed like minutes in advance Krips's eyes would seek out and lock onto the section or the solo instrument about to play, and with looks imploring, strong, or beatific, set the exact mood he wanted; meanwhile, he continued clawing the air like some giant crab. And in they came, on time, with just the right inflection and balance. Behind all of this gesturing was a jolly and wise demeanor. Of all our guest conductors that season, Krips alone offered to share his knowledge and treated us like apprentices, which I certainly was. He invited the three of us to join him for a choir rehearsal of the Beethoven Ninth at Westminster Choir School in Princeton, New Jersey. We drove out sitting face to face with him in the jump seats of a big limousine. "What have you got in your briefcase?" he asked. I pulled out my scores, and he selected Beethoven's Fifth and quickly turned to a tricky spot where the woodwinds build a pyramid, a sustained chord entered note by note, and he penciled in a longer note for the bassoon. "This is how we do it in Vienna." There were other goodies. "The last chord of every Brahms symphony is a trumpet solo!" This final weighty sounding of the tonic, an aural double bar, has stayed with me ever since and has been passed on.

Nuu?

Some of the men in the orchestra—there were no women at the time, none!—were less enthusiastic about Krips. He had conducted the summer orchestra for the Lewisohn Stadium concerts, but this was his first time on the season subscription series and I overheard several players debating whether Krips, who spent the war years in Vienna, was a Nazi sympathizer. "He must have been pro-Hitler, he was in Vienna, no?" Others said this was not so; they heard that his father was Jewish. This was in fact true, but the debate went on.[1]

Rehearsals went along normally; the naysayers kept their doubts to themselves until one morning when Krips came to a delicate entrance for a solo horn. Krips gave a little upbeat and waited, but the hornist didn't enter. Krips paused, looked over to the horn section, and said, "Nuu?" and the band laughed. From my perspective, a cloud lifted; the accusers changed their tune, and the others were pleased to be proven right. Actually, "Nuu?" proves nothing; it is commonly used in Viennese dialect. The Viennese—and the London underworld for that matter—adopted several Yiddish words and expressions well before they made their way into American English.

During one of the intermissions, as he changed into a fresh shirt and filled the room with cigar smoke—his regular routine—Krips showed me his neck chain, a star of David and a cross.

Hair

As I said, life around Bernstein was never dull. Lenny did a TV show, *The Drama of Carmen,* for which he engaged a very sexy

French mezzo-soprano, Jane Marie Andres Rhodes, nicknamed the "Bardot of the Opéra." In the hot, crowded, cable-laden TV studio we three assistant conductors were mostly in the way. So Lenny had us crouch beneath the principal cameras with vocal scores in hand ready to prompt the singers, just in case. Of course they knew the opera better than we did.

Things were going smoothly until we got to the end of the seductive *"Habanera"* when a buzzer went off and a voice from the control booth called out, "Lenny, we have to see you right away." By now you realize that I wasn't shy about being where the action is. I followed him into the booth. The playback spool was cued up and the director said, "Look at this." We watched Ms. Rhodes as she danced and sang, castanets in hand, and ended the aria in a final pose, her arms swooped up above her head. The camera freeze-framed. "See! There! Hair! We see the hair under her arms! What are we going to do?" I must say that our Carmen sported a bushy red boodle. "Who ever heard of a gypsy who shaves under her arms?" howled Lenny, and he reentered the studio and arranged a slight restaging in the interest of American sensibilities. I remained in the booth as the scene was reshot. The raunchy cameramen entertained the crowd in the director's booth by zooming in on Carmen's charms at every spare moment.

Looking back on this scene from the perspective of fifty years, I realize how far ahead of the prevailing culture Lenny was. The New York Philharmonic and television crews are no longer those all-male bastions where the mere presence of a woman, depending on her age or demeanor, evoked either chivalric respect or macho ogling and mating fantasies. At this writing, half the musicians in the Philharmonic are women. Of course it was the woman half of his bisexual self that gave Bernstein sensitivity and insights. Somehow Bernstein escaped the homophobic tauntings that Thomas Schippers, who was a guest conductor that season, received from some members of the orchestra. Bernstein was of course the music director and despite the new power of the symphony orchestra's union within a union, the ICSOM (the International Conference of Symphony and Opera Musicians, established 1962), a music director could still affect a player's career and livelihood. However, I think that Bernstein's charisma, the way he connected with people making them feel they were the only person in the room, his infectious energy and joy in music making, his deep voice and leonine good looks, made it impossible to reduce his persona to the merely sexual. I secretly dubbed him a "black hole" for attracting all the available light. Be you man, woman, or child; straight or gay; black or white; Christian, Jewish, or Muslim, Bernstein made you believe that he was a brother, sister, father, or mother, as the case required. Mind you, he was no Zelig, content with aping others as a substitute for an identity of his own. Behind the winning persona lay a fierce intelligence and a will to succeed. Moreover, Lenny had been psychoanalyzed early in his career. He knew himself well. He never got into fights he couldn't win and didn't suffer fools. That Bernstein was a loving father is attested to by his three devoted children, all of whom enjoy full lives—marriage, children, careers—and display none of the tragic neurosis we often find in the progeny of successful, world-class figures. I will say that once his wife, Felicia, died, and Helen Coates no longer held sway, the homo-hetero balance tipped in the gay direction.

Slowly I found, or placed, myself outside the inner circle, where I had fitted in quite comfortably for over twenty years.

The Glenn Gould Affair

It all started while I was at supper with the Bernstein family in their glamorous apartment at the Osborne. The phone was brought to Lenny at the table. It was Glenn Gould, who proceeded to sing and play his "bold new interpretation" of Brahms's Piano Concerto #1, in its entirety. Lenny put the phone down next to his plate and took a few bites. He murmured an occasional "aha" and "I see" into the phone and finally excused himself at a propitious moment. He then turned to me and asked, "Which one of you [assistant conductors] is covering the Brahms? I am not sure I can perform it Glenn's way." The question was strictly academic. Bernstein would need a compelling reason other than artistic differences—an illness, a death—if he really wanted out. Nevertheless his reservations about Gould's approach to the concerto were serious and the pending recording sessions for the Brahms Concerto were canceled.

On the morning of the first rehearsal, as we awaited the arrival of Mr. Gould, the stage of Carnegie Hall resembled a three-ring circus. Willy Weisel, the assistant manager of the orchestra, was whirling a hygrometer, checking the relative humidity, the parameters of which were carefully prescribed by Mr. Gould in his contract. Three Steinway concert grands crowded the stage and were getting their final tunings. Mr. Gould didn't trust making his selection in the basement of the Steinway building, where the finest concert quality instruments were stored. He would make his choice in the hall, with the orchestra. The stagehands were putting together a custom-made, collapsible, low-low stool for Mr. Gould; this perched him almost at eye level with the keyboard, and from it his hands and fingers clutched at the keys from below rather than hammering from above. Such were the goings on for this unusual soloist. But a half hour after the rehearsal was to begin, he had yet to appear.

Lenny decided to wait rather than rehearse out of order. Willy Weisel called the hotel. "There is no Mr. Gould registered there!" he reported to Lenny in his clear clipped British-cum-Viennese accent. I suggested, ever so diplomatically, that he ask for "Mr. Ockeghem," that according to a few Gould devotees I knew, Glenn Gould often registered under the name of the fifteenth-century Flemish composer. Willy tried again. "Yes, Mr. Ockeghem has left," he announced.

In a few minutes a heavily winter-coated, unkempt hulk appeared on the dressing room level. He took off his gloves—it was April—and ran hot water over his hands. He was also carrying what I guess was about an eighteen- by thirty-inch rectangle of cardboard. When Gould finally sat down before one of the Steinways, he proudly showed Lenny how he had pasted the full miniature score of the concerto on three sides of what was actually a pair of hinged boards, and that "there was only *one* turn," during the first movement. But what a turn. The cardboard swung out from the piano as Gould ducked below.

Bernstein began the introduction. Gould carefully followed the score, waving his arms, adding body English and shoulder swerves to reflect his "feeling" of the music. The tempo was glacially slow. The string players had to retake the bow at many long notes. The trills, which energize the piece, went on forever. Yet I didn't find it all that unpalatable. I like my Brahms on the slow side. But all of the *mishegas* diverted us from the music. Gould's antics had the orchestra giggling and exchanging knowing smiles.

"Well Ossip," began Harold Schonberg's review on Friday morning, a reference to the Russian pianist and conductor Ossip Gabrilovitch, son-in-law to Mark Twain, "who would have believed it?" Schonberg then proceeded to take Bernstein to task for reading an *apologia* to the audience *before* the performance, admitting that while he disagreed with Gould's interpretation, he would nevertheless conduct out of respect for Gould the artist. I was in Lenny's dressing room moments before the first performance, as he previewed the *apologia* for several of his friends, including Carlos Moseley, the very proper southern gentleman who was the manager of the New York Philharmonic. "Don't do it! Lenny, please!" argued Carlos. But Lenny had the bit in his mouth. He couldn't resist the excitement he knew this would generate. I, too, wanted him to let it rip. What the hell.

What would have been just another tried and true, predictable week on the Philharmonic concert season turned into a fun-filled media event. Meanwhile, the interpretive distance between Bernstein and Gould narrowed, and a reconciliation took place before their last performance that went largely unnoticed. Gould and Lenny were about to go onstage for the final Sunday afternoon performance of the Brahms. I stood nearby. Lenny took a last puff of his cigarette and turned to Gould. "Glenn, I've done it your way three times now, let's try mine." Gould nodded and said, "Okay." They went out all smiles and the performance of the Brahms sounded like so many others before or since.

Although the half-life of the "debacle" has long since passed, I still come across Gould fanciers who claim that it was because of the Bernstein/Brahms brouhaha that Gould gave up live performance. This is not so. I heard about a performance of the Brahms by Gould shortly after the Bernstein encounter—I think it was with the Baltimore Symphony. He played the piano they provided. There were no antics with the giant score, no hygrometer, and the tempi were "normal." A selection of New York Philharmonic historic performances was issued on CD in 1999, among them, the third performance of the Bernstein/Gould collaboration, the Saturday night radio broadcast. Those Gould mavens who remember the saga got out their watches and metronomes only to find that the performance falls well within the range of timings and tempi we have grown to expect.[2]

Mentorship

For the young conductor who is moving from talented student to professional, the ideal path is to have a mentor—to work closely with a master performer, making oneself useful for any and all musical tasks from marking bowings to conducting the occasional acoustic run-through, and being able to observe one's mentor interacting with top professional orchestras and soloists. It offers opportunities for invaluable off-the-podium talks, and hopefully, well-placed recommendations.

Lenny rarely sat with we three assistant conductors to walk us through a score. He never did when I worked on *West Side Story, Candide,* or *Mass.* The only suggestion I remember him giving me much later was to open the ever popular *Candide* Overture slightly under tempo for the opening fanfares and let 'er rip into a lightning-fast tempo on the descending scale. Oh yes, and to "just stand there, and let it happen," for my Satie's *Parade.*

We assistants had access to Bernstein's dressing room and heard him interact with librarians, his personnel manager, program note annotator, and even Carlos Moseley, the orchestra's manager. The height of my learning experience was in watching him and the orchestra through every rehearsal, as they brought pieces to perfection—that is where we learned about the details in the score that needed attention—and in hearing the orchestra grow from performance to performance (the critics always came too soon), and being able to interact with some of the players. I also observed Bernstein in the green room after the concert, his personal assistant Helen Coates just behind, slipping him names as important people approached, and his intense eye-to-eye conversations with young musicians or old friends; I watched as Lenny tuned out everyone else in the room and spoke absolute *emmes* (life-reinforcing truths) one on one with someone who was, or was about to become, a committed Bernstein supporter for life.

Form

Bernstein asked me to run through a Haydn Minuet during a camera rehearsal of a Young People's Concert. After the show was taped, we were relaxing backstage and he asked me why I made a ritard at the end of the trio. "It was the recapitulation," I replied. He began to sing, "The re-capit-u-*lay*-tion, the re-capit-u-*lay*-tion," as he hopped about the room in time. Bernstein was letting me know in an entertaining and unforgettable way that "telegraphing" what was about to happen is not a good idea. A concert is not a theory lesson.

Many artists are aware of structure while they are playing, where they are and where they are going in the evolving form of a classic work, and they consciously incorporate this into their performance. The question remains whether the *audience,* the *listeners,* need be made aware of form, and whether it enhances their "understanding" or pleasure. I for one refuse to believe that Beethoven, master architect that he was, expected his audience to be *consciously* analyzing form or structure—"Sally, dear, are we still in the development?"—any more than the master architects of Chartres Cathedral wanted us to be aware of the flying buttresses that made the soaring glass and stone edifice possible. I have never heard someone commenting after a concert, "Did you notice the delayed recapitulation, the second theme on the mediant rather than the subdominant?"

The notion "that art should be experienced viscerally rather than cerebrally" was championed by the celebrated woman of letters Susan Sontag in her first collection of essays, *Against Interpretation and Other Essays.*[3] Certainly we all respond to the comforting return of a principal melody after a long journey—with pleasure when anticipated, or admiration when unexpected. And yes, Beethoven took great pains—we know how hard he labored from his voluminous sketchbooks—and must have derived great satisfaction, as he exploited his motifs, blowing them up, turning them this way and that. But he *always* had the ears of his audience in mind. Are we not drawn in, bit by bit, by the dramatic and mysterious opening of his Ninth Symphony as the elements of his heroic theme are revealed, the dropping fourths and fifths waiting for a resolution; will it be in major or minor? And are we not diverted, as the movement draws to a close, by his deeply moving *cortege* over a ground bass while he cunningly builds his rhythmic cell into a final triumphant bursting forth of that same heroic theme?

Great music demands our total attention and engages us completely in an *aural, emotional* journey. The conductor, who guides us on this journey, may have benefited from the theoretician's systematic parsing and deconstruction of the compositional process when the classic sonata-allegro form held sway. But this sturdy model for musical art has long past. Composers found other, more appropriate, ways to organize their works. When conducting Debussy, a composer who firmly rejected classic "Germanic" structures, I seek his unique and, for his time, refreshing "French" atmosphere and color—elegant and transparent, yet never sentimental or weak-kneed.[4]

I luxuriate in his unique use of extended harmonies, *chords* enjoyed, danced upon for their own sake, and let Debussy's "evolving form" take care of itself. Bartok, too, requires trust. I wend my way, exploiting his exotic tunes and spiky rhythms, his dances and fugues, and when the "golden section" moment arrives I revel in his immense tutti celebrations.[5]

With Ellington, I try above all to swing, giving over to the rhythm section the husbanding of time. Under their kinetic spell you can sharply cue the band, lining up tuttis and tightening call-and-response figures; Duke prodded the band with piano punctuations, carefully placed *comp* chords, and when it was called for, he would rise from his piano bench and conduct. I heartily bend "blue" notes and encourage the truly original improvisers to fly and, conversely, monitor those who are reconstructing famous Ben Webster or Tricky Sam Nanton solos—and let Duke's endless expansions of the blues form speak for themselves.

Bernstein once thought out loud to me that he sought common metric relationships between adjacent movements of a classical symphony—an overall tactus, a planetary pull that binds the constellation of movements to one another. For example, a pulse that is established in the first movement for an entire measure can be carried into the slower second movement as the pulse for a single quarter note. It can be posited that Mozart and Puccini built an overall pulse, a tempo relationship, into entire operatic acts. Think of Act Two, *Boheme.* The pulse and energy of the trumpet fanfare that starts us off are carried—or can be carried—throughout the movement, even into Musetta's waltz aria. If you like coherence, continuity, these are useful ideas. If you are drawn to angular juxtapositions, or welcome surprises—like those provided by the master architect Frank Lloyd Wright when his narrow, low-ceilinged hallways spill into dramatic open spaces—these ideas are less attractive. Once again Bernstein was enlisting his composer's instinct. Just as he sifted through banal passages, searching for nuggets of value, he sought coherence by organizing discrete movements into longer shapes through the use of time.

Bernstein was very attentive to bowings. He would demand a *quiet* intensity by asking the players to use a *"forte* left hand and a *piano* bow [hand]." He would sometimes ask the violins and violas to break, or spread out, triple-stop and quadruple-stop chords, like the one we hear at the start of Beethoven's First Symphony. "Ga-*hoy!*" he would call out, imitating the expressive two-part stroke, the sound of the lower string's preparation *before* the beat, and the rest of the chord *on* the beat, rather than the more common, knife-like, percussive chunk.

During the last summer of Leonard Bernstein's life he was scheduled to perform the Beethoven Seventh with the Boston Symphony at his beloved Tanglewood. It was perhaps his fiftieth-plus performance. He recorded it with the New York and the Vienna Philharmonic. One would assume that Bernstein had long ago worked out every nuance and bowing to his satisfaction. But in fact he never stopped searching for a better way, a most important message for me as an artist. I got this story from a young librarian friend of mine, Adam Zeichner, who spent days preparing a new set of bowings and marked parts from Lenny's freshly marked score for the Tanglewood performance that would be his last.

What was most remarkable for me about Bernstein's conducting was the way he would energize a mundane passage. Rather than rushing through, getting it over with—a dead giveaway—Bernstein would often spend time exploring, underlining a dissonance or a rhythm, playing with the dynamics, keeping the band and the audience involved. On the other hand he was not beyond making a cut when he thought it would enhance a work, even in the presence of a celebrated composer like Copland, whose Third Symphony and *Fanfare for the Common Man* received trimmings, as did David Diamond's Ninth Symphony and Roy Harris's Third Symphony.

In one of my last conversations with my mentor, backstage after a New York Philharmonic concert, having been asked how things were, I said that I was "mostly teaching these days," thinking, "*Get me some GIGS!*" Bernstein launched into a speech: "What are we but teachers, maestros? I'm teaching all the time. Do you think the New York Philharmonic knew *Francesca da Rimini* before tonight? No! I had to teach it to them bar by bar." They learned well. I was blown away by how Lenny drove the orchestra into a dazzlingly virtuoso performance that night. It sounded as if they had been playing *Francesca da Rimini* all their lives. And it was best I find my own way, which I did.

6

Are You Jewish?

♪

ometime in the second half of my Philharmonic year
Bernstein or Helen Coates, I cannot remember who,
set up a meeting for me with Arthur Judson, head of
Columbia Artists Management.

When I walked into his offices across the street from Carnegie
Hall, I was warmly greeted by a robust eighty-year-old man sitting
in a Boston rocker. I had no idea that before he was investigated
by the FBI and the FCC, and sued by the US Attorney General,
Arthur Judson controlled an amalgamation of seven independent
concert bureaus that managed 125 artists and organizations, ap-
proximately two-thirds of the top musicians in America. He was
the second largest shareholder of the Columbia Broadcasting
System (thereby influencing its subsidiary, Columbia Records,
Bernstein's label) and only six years earlier stepped down as board
chairman of the New York Philharmonic.

His first question was, "Are you Jewish?" I bridled, thinking,
"These were fighting words when I was growing up." I was married
to a nominal Christian woman, my name was not Jewish sounding,

I had served in the army. I was an American. Jewish was not at the top of my ID list, or so I thought at the time. I could pass. What does it matter? Judson explained that I was a potential music director and there were cities that were happy with a Jewish conductor and those that were not, acknowledging the presence of a pervasive bigotry in parts of America. In fact Bernstein had bitterly confided in me that "the Boston Symphony would never accept a Jewish conductor," meaning himself—Boston-born, Harvard standout, Koussevitzky protégé, Tanglewood hero; ironically, Boston was about to engage Erich Leinsdorf, born Erich Landauer from a Jewish family in Vienna.

When next I saw Bernstein I asked him, "Who is this guy, Judson, asking me about my religion?" "That's nothing. Koussevitzky told me," and he imitated a Yiddish accent, "Mit da name Boinshtine, a chob [job] you'll never hev." Like almost all Jewish-born conductors of his generation, Bernstein's mentor, Koussevitzky, had converted. Many changed their names. He expected Lenny to do the same. But those sad days were over, or at least I assumed so until I met Judson.

Judson moved on to discuss building a career. Before I left he signed me to a contract, and I became a Columbia Artist. Sitting in on the conversation and taking notes was Ronald Wilford, who at this writing is one of the most powerful artist managers in the music world. He would be my personal manager at Columbia Artists for the next three years.

So—despite the Arthur Judsons of the world who went along cynically exploiting rather than fighting anti-Semitism, we have to thank Bernstein, who by keeping his good Jewish name was helping break the shameful self-denial once and for all.

In my lifetime I witnessed all the walls of sexism and false moral shame crumble. We now have openly gay conductors well out of the proverbial "closet," and women conductors leading major orchestras and presiding in opera houses. Former Communists write about their youthful idealism. We have a black president, twice elected.

But where do I now stand as a musician born into the first "it's okay to be Jewish" generation? In the process of writing this memoir I realized my trying to have an ecumenical, label-free life and career with music as my faith was made possible, imaginable, inevitably fashioned, by my Jewish core. When I dive deeper into my guts—my *kishkes*—I see my curious Middle Eastern and European mix of Jewishness as a gift, a moral compass, an inherent outsiderness, written about by Freud in *Moses and Monotheism*,[1] that often prepares one "as it would eventually prepare others in the West—[with] an advantage in all activities that involved making an abstract model of experience, in words or numbers or lines, and working with the abstraction to achieve control over nature or to bring humane order to life." Freud calls this internalizing process an "advance in intellectuality," and he credits it directly to religion. "The mental labor of monotheism prepared the Jews to achieve distinction in law, in mathematics, in science and in literary art."[2]

Naturally I have been curious about the outcomes, the price paid, by so many Jewish-born musicians who converted or came to deny their origins.

There is no major figure in the history of music whose work suffered a stronger suppression of its greatness than Felix Mendelssohn. At its root is a virulent anti-Semitism triggered and sustained by Richard Wagner and embraced by the German-speaking musical community up through the Holocaust; it is only now in the process of being righted by scholars. I stopped conducting Wagner once I started teaching at the Aaron Copland School of Music. He chose to introduce his megalomaniacal philosophy, a radical politics of bigotry and racism, into his music and writings. I can no longer separate the two.

Wagner's dream of a Jewish-free Germany almost came to fruition with the Nazi takeover. Thousands of Jewish musicians ended their lives in concentration camps, as did my mother's family. The lucky ones, a legion of accomplished people with Jewish ancestry, fled from the opera houses, academies, and publishing houses of Germany and eastern Europe. Many came to America, including almost all my teachers at the Mannes School, and my favorite, Curt Sachs, at NYU. Among them are several conductors who became the musical models for my generation, gracing the podiums of Cleveland, Chicago, and New York, namely, George Szell, Fritz Reiner, and Bruno Walter—thus Arthur Judson's provocative question for me.

Meanwhile, what would become known as the Holocaust forced a fierce "coming out" that happened all around me. Unabashedly literal Jewish themes and texts appeared in the music of Arnold Schoenberg, Kurt Weill, and a very young Leonard Bernstein. Schoenberg, father of atonal music, who had converted to Catholicism following the lead of his hero Gustav Mahler, made a symbolic return to the fold in 1938 with his Hebrew setting of *Kol Nidrei*; the opening "declaration" for the Day of Atonement excuses those who have strayed from the faith and welcomes them to join in prayer. At Bernstein's suggestion I have championed another Schoenberg

Jewish-inspired work, "A Survivor from Warsaw," a dramatic setting of an uprising in the same ghetto where my mother's family disappeared. In 1937 Kurt Weill wrote the music for *The Eternal Road,* an opera-oratorio that combined biblical and pre–World War II Jewish history. It was performed 153 times at the Manhattan Opera House; Franz Werfel composed the libretto, Max Reinhard directed, Lotte Lenya sang the role of Miriam, and thirteen-year-old Sydney Lumet was a boy tenor. I have often performed Bernstein's First Symphony for Orchestra and Mezzo-soprano, composed in 1943. Painfully aware of the death camps in Poland and Germany, Bernstein, at age twenty-five, followed the biblical story of Jeremiah from the *Book of Lamentations.* It opens with a powerful and unsettling movement, a cry of pain. The second movement converts the blessings of the Torah and Haftorah, chanted at every bat-bar mitzvah, into a wild Hassidic dance. The finale is a setting of the tragic, metaphoric biblical text, sung in Hebrew, here translated:

> The cry of Jeremiah as he mourns his beloved Jerusalem, ruined, pillaged and dishonored after his desperate effort to save it. . . . How doth the city sit solitary that was full of people! How she has become as a widow! . . . She weepeth sore into the night. . . . She has none to comfort her among all her lovers. Wherefore dost Thou forget us for ever?

A Story of Acoustical Tests

My New York Philharmonic season is coming to an end. The orchestra has been moved to their soon-to-be new hall at Lincoln Center for five days of acoustical tests. It is morning of day one, May 28, 1962. Seiji Ozawa has just finished leading the orchestra in a section from Brahms Symphony #3 and I am about to lead Ravel's gorgeously orchestrated "Dawn" from his Daphnis and Chloe Suite #2. I gently start the woodwinds and harps bubbling over a whisper of held string chords in harmonics. The basses start deep on their lowest string, a slow rising theme climbs through the cellos and violas, the violins carry it higher as shepherd pipes and birdlike tweets and twitters greet the dawn. The brass swells and you can actually hear the sun coming out. What genius. What a thrill.

Lenny had done the work earlier in the season. I never saw a score with so many notes, some pages were almost black, but I studied hard and the piece was now moving nicely. I think to myself, "Stay out of their way, adjust the tempos as the oboe trio enters, and listen, listen, damn it! Beat small; it's a huge orchestra yielding gentle and delicate sounds." It was apparent that the orchestra sounded richer, warmer, in Carnegie, home to the Philharmonic for almost seventy years. "Maybe I should make them play louder, slower, faster ..."

John Canarina takes over with Beethoven's Fourth Piano Concerto, Malcolm Frager at the Steinway. I walk into the deep and lofty hall to listen. Adjustable "clouds" hang from the ceiling, an idea borrowed from the Tanglewood shed, which boasts better-than-usual acoustics for an outdoor concert space. Folded into the seats were fiberglass battens, "the sound absorption equivalent of a human body." What sound? Where is the sound? Our sound?

Bernstein sometimes spoke to me in Yiddish. One of his favorite maxims, "helfen vi a toyten bankes" ("helpful as cupping a corpse"), describes the search for an acceptable acoustic that would continue throughout the week; whole sections of the orchestra were moved about, closer, farther, on risers, on the floor. By midweek everyone present became painfully aware to what degree Carnegie Hall held the sonic soul of this great orchestra. Bill Vacchiano, first trumpeter, and one of my former teachers, confided, "I created my sound in Carnegie Hall; what will I do now?" Bernstein visited to listen and left after a half hour knowing the hall was a bust. By the end of the week, Leopold Stokowski, a renowned sound-sorcerer, was asked to conduct. Everyone agreed, "He will know what to do." Stoki waved away the sheaf of scores that were being tested. "Gentlemen, the first two chords of the *Eroica*. Trombones and tuba, you, too, E-flat!" Whap ... whap! went the orchestra. He paused a moment to listen. "It will never do!" Prophetic words said aloud; Stoki continued mumbling to himself as he left the stage, "They should have called me before they built it."[3]

Thanks to the acoustical tests, my life was about to change; Janet Harte, the wife of the president of the Corpus Christi Symphony, came one afternoon to see me in action. Their music director, Jacques Singer, had left suddenly and my new management, Columbia Artists, recommended me for the post. I already turned down an offer from the Harvard-Radcliffe student orchestra ("We do not offer tenure, but Harvard is a nice place to be from"). My first mentor, Martin Bernstein, chair of the NYU Music Department, assumed I would be moving on after the

Philharmonic assistantship and arranged for someone else to take over my orchestra and courses. I had no plans beyond the coming summer of 1962, when I would be music director of the Hyannis Melody Tent.

At lunch with Janet Harte it was reassuring to learn she was a New Englander and a graduate of Bennington College—she would eventually help sponsor our daughter Lorca to attend Bennington as well. Mrs. Harte told me positive things about Corpus Christi, and how well it supported their part-time professional orchestra. A few days later I flew down to Texas to meet the board and they offered me the post. The soloists that first season had already been chosen; they would include several stars including Benny Goodman, a good omen. I discussed my mostly positive impressions with Gloria, and after weighing our options, she gave her reluctant approval and we took an immense, adventurous leap. We would be crossing the Hudson—as drawn in Sol Steinberg's xenophobic map of America—a *wide sea* between Manhattan and Los Angeles and everywhere in between, moving our family, Lorca, age four, and Paul, age two, and our few possessions far from the happenings and outdoor art shows, the Sunday hootenannies around the Washington Square fountain only a few steps from our home, from the counterculture of Greenwich Village to what was then a balmy, rather beautiful semitropical Tex-Mex town on the Gulf of Mexico.

I would have my own orchestra. Thanks to the GI Bill we would own a home. My salary was the equivalent of over $90,000 in 2013 dollars. The president of CAMI cheered me on: "Build a better orchestra in Texas," and they would "move me up the ladder." In those prefeminist days it was assumed that Father's career came first. Gloria completed her bachelor's degree in Corpus. She wrote poetry and, coming from a Puerto Rican family, enjoyed using her mother tongue in that bilingual city. We made new friends and lived life—soon Anika Toba, our third child, would bring immense joy to us all.

Dianu, it would have been enough had my NY Philharmonic year been the last I would see of Bernstein. I had absorbed so much and was eager to put it to work. But we would continue to work together, and I would continue to learn from him, over the next two decades.

7
A Music Director in Texas I

♪

I inherited an enviable roster of solo artists for my first season in Corpus Christi. It included the pianists Julius Katchen, Arthur Brailovsky, and the duo-piano team Gold and Fizdale, and three legendary instrumentalists, the already mentioned clarinetist Benny Goodman, classical guitarist Andres Segovia, and violinist Mischa Elman. These were the informed choices of my predecessor, Jacques Singer.

Mischa Elman arrived under the impression that I was Jacques Singer. "Mr. Zingeh, tell me, vere ken vee eat tonight?" In my youthful eagerness, before I came to the realization that getting too familiar with an artist in advance of making music together was a fatal error, I would meet them at the airport. "I know a nice seafood restaurant with a fine view of the bay," I offered, without correcting him on my name. "I'll be happy to drive you there."

As we studied the menu he asked me where I was from. I told him that I had spent a season with Bernstein, as an assistant conductor with the Philharmonic. "Mr. Zingeh, I played with the New York Philharmonic every year for forty seasons, until that lousy Mr. Bernshtayne arrived." It was an awkward moment. I mumbled something like, "Why yes, you should have played, let me see, we had Francescotti last season and—" "Mr. Zingeh," he interrupted, "you can mention one other violinist in my presence. [pause] Francescotti is not the one. I will eat alone if you do not mind." And he moved to another table for the entire meal. Afterwards I drove him to his hotel.

The next time we met was onstage for the orchestra rehearsal. I had scheduled the Mendelssohn Concerto, which normally stands on its own, but Elman insisted on doing a Vivaldi Concerto in D minor as an encore. With his added schmaltz and throbbing vibrato, Vivaldi sounded like one of the Russian-Yiddish lullabies my mother used to sing to me. I remember his impatience during the rehearsal of the Mendelssohn. Every time the orchestra had a tutti passage, something of its own to play, he would walk up and down the violins shouting, "More bow, more bow!" Then came the concert. I was walking behind Elman as we were about to enter the stage and, being much taller than his five foot two or three, I gave him some space. I had been well drilled by Helen Coates in the hard and fast rules of concert etiquette, that I be the gracious host, but I almost walked over Elman when he suddenly stopped our advance at the curtain trim on the edge of the stage, thrust his acclaimed Tiger Stripe Strad ahead of him where it could be seen, and waited for applause to begin. He then stepped before the audience, again pausing for effect, and only when the applause grew did he finally start walking toward the podium and the soloist's position, the Tiger Stripe Strad still outstretched before him. I have done the Mendelssohn with several master violinists since

1962, and find it a joyful and aristocratic work that calls for a deft and light accompaniment. Lord only knows how I approached it as a journeyman conductor with Elman breathing down my neck.

Elman was immortalized by the Gershwins in their 1921 spoof song about four Russian-Jewish violinists, "Mischa, Yascha, Toscha, Sascha," a time when Elman was the pride and joy of the great concert impresario Sol Hurok, who spoke to me about him when I first visited his offices: "My first artist, we traveled by coal-fired steam locomotive. Wherever it stopped we got off. We were so covered with soot we looked like Negroes. I put up signs on every pole and billboard, 'Mischa Elman, the world's greatest violinist will play tonight.' And we packed them in. That's how I, Hurok, started my career—with Mischa, following the train routes from one one-horse-town to another." This story dates to around 1912, soon after Hurok and Elman immigrated to the States from Russia.

I was reminded of Elman's "More bow!" outburst years later, in 1993, when I came across an Elman edition—his particular bowings and phrasings—of a work for solo violin and piano by Reuben Goldmark, "The Call of the Plains." When I compared Elman's markings with the same phrases in Goldmark's orchestral version of the piece, I realized how effectively Elman "carved" out and sculpted the melody with many adroit changes of up and down bows—the musical equivalent of an actor's emphasizing consonants to propel the vowels. I eagerly copied Elman's bowings into the orchestral parts. I learned a great deal from Elman.

There were a few other clashes of will that season: with Benny Goodman, who I have since found out was a notorious grouch, and with Segovia, who had become paranoid that his guitar, the most intimate of instruments, would not be heard when he worked with an orchestra, no matter how tiny the band or how delicately they played. It was my introduction to the acting out of insecurities and fears by even the most seasoned and established master performers, and to the real world of concert giving. Goodman finally agreed to honor his contract and play at our Young People's Concert, but only after I threatened to cancel the whole engagement. Had he disappointed the eager Corpus Christi mothers and their charges—they had already bought out every seat in the Bayfront Coliseum—my credibility as the new music director would have been sorely compromised. As it turned out Goodman's interpretation of the Mozart Clarinet Concerto, "play it like opera," was one of the memorable Mozart lessons of my young life.

Segovia shot a warning glare at the band as he entered the stage for rehearsal, but they smiled back in return and hardly touched bow to string or breathed air into their flutes and horns as they accompanied him in the Mario Castelnuevo-Tedesco Concerto. Almost fifty years later, in 2011, I received an email about the Segovia concert from Fred Schock, the principal clarinetist back then. He recalled "playing so softly I couldn't hear myself." And went on to write, "Well, 'the man' stopped for a second time and told the conductor that the winds 'are playing like a bunch of pigs' at which point the conductor said 'I refuse to let you talk that way to my musicians.' When Segovia refused to apologize, the conductor walked off the stage and so did Segovia."

I remember storming off to find my manager, Mrs. Litta Kline, who made him offer some apology and, according to Fred, the performance the next day was well received and it all ended happily.

In time I developed the necessary "elephant skin" and learned to laugh off provocative comments. In our second season Eileen Farrell sang Wagner's *Wesondonck Lieder* and the Immolation Scene from *Gotterdammerung*—clearly I had not yet reached my more informed position on Wagner—the same works she sang at the beginning of my year with the Philharmonic, and we had fun. I prided myself with being in perfect synch with soloists. Yet at our rehearsal there was a moment when Farrell held on to a final fading note well after I cut off the orchestra. "Eileen," I said, "won't you cut off with the orchestra?" Quick as a whip she replied, "They paid to hear me." The players laughed, but it was an open challenge to *Maestro*; I could have objected, but I quickly realized there was musical wisdom in her response. And ever since, at similar musical moments, I have asked soloists, fiddlers and clarinetists, as well as singers, to let their sound extend a bit beyond the orchestra's, so that the solo line remains the last thing we hear, remains uppermost—a useful music lesson.

Eileen had a foul mouth and loved to tell musician stories, including one I cannot resist sharing. She told me about being a soloist in the Bach Aria Group with the Metropolitan Opera star tenor Jan Peerce. Peerce nailed a high A at one of their concerts, a perfectly focused, shining note. After the applause he sat down next to Eileen and she said, "That was magnificent. How did you do that?" Peerce answered, "It's easy. I make believe someone is shoving an ice cream cone up my ass!" A few days passed and Peerce sang another aria with a stirring, rafter-shaking high note.

After he sat Eileen leaned over and whispered, "Chocolate or vanilla?" That's Eileen.

Eilleen Farrell sang Isolde in a concert performance of Wagner's *Tristan und Isolde* with the Kansas City Philharmonic at the Kennedy Center in January 1977 with Jess Thomas as Tristan. Eileen surprised us with a thrilling *ossia* (optional) high C in the second act. As we hugged during final bows she whispered, "That was my last Isolde!" A few years passed and Eileen started teaching at the Indiana University School of Music. And with her big Irish smile and even grander still gorgeous voice she started giving concerts of pop tunes, what became known as the Great American Songbook. We booked her on the Pop Series in Kansas City and I asked my excellent assistant conductor, Frank Collura, who normally did the pop series, to let me conduct for her. I even accompanied her at the piano (my concert keyboard debut) in an encore, "My Funny Valentine." Lucky us, from Richard Wagner to Richard Rodgers in one lifetime.

Kaddish for Kennedy

The event that would shape my career forever occurred in 1963, my third season in Corpus Christi when President Kennedy was assassinated in Dallas. I remember cursing out the rednecks whose hostility to his visit I had read about that morning. I drove home and Gloria was crying. We had no TV—we wanted Lorca and Paul to grow up reading books—but I immediately rented one and we followed the sad saga, glued to the beast with the rest of the country. Bernstein was in his Fairfield, Connecticut, studio working on his Kaddish Symphony, which was originally intended to honor his father "while he's still alive!" when the awful news came. He immediately changed its dedication to John F. Kennedy.

Lenny and his wife, Felicia, who had a theatrical career as Felicia Montealegre, knew the Kennedys. Helen Coates spoke of play dates between the Bernstein and Kennedy children and I remember Lenny's mischievous story about a dinner party at the Kennedy White House: "Stravinsky fell asleep in his soup, and we all went upstairs to dance the twist!"

In the spring of 1964 I traveled up from Texas to attend Lenny's rehearsals, performances, and recording sessions of his Kaddish Symphony with the New York Philharmonic. The work was huge and complicated: two choirs, extra-large orchestra, soprano soloist, and narrator. I left fired up with the idea that my Texas orchestra and Texan choirs must perform this work on, or close to, the first anniversary of the Kennedy tragedy.

I hoped that Felicia, who narrated the New York performances, would do the same in Corpus, but according to her manager at Columbia Artists, she was "unavailable." My guess is she was probably skeptical about what might happen in the wilds of south Texas. And so we engaged, in her place, Patricia Neway, who had made a distinguished career as a singer—she created the role of Magda Sorel in Menotti's opera *The Consul*—but by that time she was appearing more often as a dramatic actress. Our big concert choir came from North Texas State University, near Dallas. I formed and trained a children's choir in Corpus. Like the city, it was a vibrant mix of brown-skinned Mexican and "Anglo" kids, and included Lorca, age seven. Hearing them sing the complicated rhythms, in Hebrew, by heart, their trusting eyes never leaving me, is one of my treasured memories. The performance on November 16, 1964, was our own Texas Kaddish for Kennedy. I found that a transcendent performance, one in which the audience and musicians lose themselves in the embrace of a masterwork, could take place in Del Mar Auditorium as well as at Lincoln Center. When and why such moments occur is one of life's mysteries. But it did for the Kaddish Symphony.

Lenny and Felicia were, for obvious reasons, curious to hear the tape of our performance. We listened to it together while lying on rugs in front of the fire in the library of their Park Avenue penthouse apartment. They were both overwhelmed and grabbed me at the end. Lenny took me out to dinner and told everyone, the waiters, the people at the next table, "This is Maurice Peress. He just did my Kaddish Symphony and it was glorious."

Bernstein began to call on me to conduct his music, *Candide* in Chicago, *West Side Story* at Lincoln Center. He or Helen Coates also recommended me for the codirectorship of a fascinating music and dance pilot project for the Bureau of Indian Affairs (BIA).

My Indian Year

The call came from a BIA public relations person: "We are looking for a project director, preferably American Indian, to lead a new music program for the Bureau of Indian Affairs. " I said nothing and he continued, "Being that you are of Mexican origin [he read Peress as Perez] and from Texas we thought you might be our man." I replied, "I only have one word for you: Shalom!" He evidently was charmed by my response and began talking about the program. I found it intriguing. Believe me, had I known any American Indian musicians at the time I would have been happy to refer them to him. My ignorance was complete. We left it that I would do some serious digging and get back to him. Only years later did I realize that I was about to make my first sortie into Dvorak territory.

In the then current *Grove's Dictionary of Music and Musicians* (fifth edition, 1954), I found only a single bleak line about American-Indian music: "We accept the proposition that ... American-Indian traditions are isolated, fragmentary and probably recessive." However, in an earlier edition of *Grove's* (third edition, 1927, American Supplement), I found a sizeable article replete with engaging details, such as the establishment by American composers of the Wa-Wan Press, who "following Dvorak's lead" saw in Indian music a resource for their own compositions. Why had there been, in so short a time, a reversal of interest in the music of American Indians?

The Secretary of the Interior, Stewart Udall, and his wife, Lee, had envisioned a project close to their hearts, to reinforce and support the study of traditional Native American music and dance in BIA schools that were scattered throughout Arizona and New Mexico. They wanted to do something that would reverse the attrition of native culture brought on by decades of conflicting BIA policy. Since it was first established under the Department of the Interior in 1849, the Bureau flip-flopped between benign neglect toward the Indians' threatened cultural traditions—the reservation approach—and trying to hasten acculturation by requiring all Indian children to attend BIA boarding schools where they were taught "the American way." Being Mormons, the Udalls were particularly aware of the dangers of cultural arrogance, for the Latter Day Saints had long supported a conversion program, sending their young black-suited, bible-toting sons onto the reservations to save the Indian soul.

I began compiling a list of Indian-inspired works for small and large ensembles. I searched for musicians with some American Indian heritage, and found among them Sammy Mayes (after maize, the Indian name for corn), the grandson of a Cherokee chief and until 1964 the principal cellist of the Boston Symphony; jazz pianist/composer John Lewis; Chandler Goetting, first trumpet of the Sante Fe Opera; and the composer Louis Ballard. Ballard, who lived in Santa Fe, New Mexico, directed a novel music program in the local BIA school: a singing, dancing, and drumming choir that gave dramatic performances of tribal music he cleverly joined into substantial set pieces.

I visited the BIA offices in Washington, DC, to seriously explore the idea of becoming their music project director. I was confident that I could design a series of "show and tell" concerts that would fulfill some of the project's objectives, concerts that would include Indian tribal music and "classical" works derived from this source, such as "Scenes from Indian Life" by Ballard and music from the standard repertoire that featured Native American soloists. I shared my ideas with an excited project staff at the BIA offices. But when Louis Ballard's name came up, there were exasperated "here we go again" reactions.

Although there was a time when the BIA administrators took pride in Ballard's choir and were quite eager to show it off, he had become a thorn in their side. Ballard was an artist, not a bureaucrat, and his constant lobbying for commissions for himself as a composer and for his noble dream, an Institute of American Indian Arts, only succeeded in reminding the BIA folks in Washington how ineffective and uninformed they were when it came to the arts. It became apparent to me that one of the reasons the BIA went to the Bernstein office for a recommendation was to get around Ballard and his "pushy" Brooklyn-born wife, Ruth, who spurred him on. I could not play along and I told them I had to meet Ballard and see if he could be persuaded to join the "Music Committee," the team of experts we would need to advise us and help legitimize the project. They agreed to send me to Santa Fe.

When the door to the Ballard house opened, I was immediately attacked by a furious Ruth Ballard: "How dare you think you can direct this program," she snarled. "You're not Indian." I was now the focus of their frustrations, Mr. BIA himself. "Louis is the only one who is qualified; this is just another Big Horn massacre." She shouted me into the living room, where Louis Ballard, a huge hulk of a man whose sheepish grin did little to disguise how much he was enjoying her onslaught, awaited with a bottle of bourbon and a glass. I'm a scotch drinker but I gratefully accepted the offer. Slowly I explained how much the project needed him, that I would be his buffer with the BIA, that whoever was the director wasn't important, we would be partners, that there was a greater responsibility to the culture, which I respected, and lastly—the real clincher—I would commission Louis to compose several works at good fees. Ballard joined the team.

In the early spring of 1968, I was taken on an orientation tour of Indian communities in Arizona and New Mexico by Lee Udall, who was familiar with the area and knew many of its people. A small chartered plane landed us on dusty strips near the Pima, Navaho, and Zuni reservations. We stopped overnight in awesomely inspiring Monument Valley, Utah. A young doctor who ran a clinic for the local Indians showed me his collection of native artifacts, which included mourner's tear cups, tiny fired-clay bowls that the Indians buried with their dead. He told me about the unusual birthmarks on the backs of newborn Navaho babies that are common to Korean and Japanese babies as well. As he talked on, I was made uncomfortable by his obsessive curiosity. He was dangerously close to becoming what politically aware Indians label an "anthro" man. I would have to guard myself against this kind of voyeurism.

Learning even a little about Indian people and their ways inspired in me a growing respect. For example, the band director at a BIA boarding school in Phoenix told me that when he first arrived he followed the normal practice of auditioning the players before choosing a student to be principal clarinetist or trumpeter, but they would refuse the honor. Tribal traditions, he soon learned, required that the students select their own leaders by acclamation. Invariably, they made the best choice.

On the Pima Reservation, the poorest and most depressing of all that we visited, the reservation director listened patiently as Mrs. Udall and I waxed on about the year ahead: "There will be chamber music and teachers' workshops and a visit by the Phoenix Symphony." "Mister," he replied, "tell them we need blankets." I always trot out this story for my conservative friends as an example of the perils of governing from afar. I was humbled and embarrassed to think that my normal enthusiasm for creating musical events could make me appear arrogant.

I learned that Indian music is without artifice; it is prayer, history, an accompaniment and enhancement for work and courtship, and for tribal dances. Songs come to one in a dream or trance. They must be inherited or passed on as a gift. Ballard taught me that Indians have their own protocol for passing on a song. The keeper or bearer of a song waits patiently until the learner has absorbed all of its nuances. It then becomes the new owner's responsibility, literally a "copyright," to carry and protect and pass on in turn.

Willard Rhodes, ethnomusicologist and Columbia University professor (and conductor of *The Barrier* performance that so influenced me!) joined Louis Ballard and me to complete the Music Committee. In late June of 1968, we gathered in Albuquerque and Santa Fe for a summit pow-wow with José Limón and Martha Hill who together led the Dance Committee. Limón was impressive, a man of unusual beauty inside and out. My memory of him evokes earth and sculpture, balance and cheer. I recently came across a convocation speech that Limón delivered in 1968, shortly after our summit meeting and that by good fortune has been published.[1]

Limón recounts an experience we shared during our big BIA pow-wow, a tribal ceremonial at the ancient pueblo of San Felipe. He entitled it "On Magic."

In the plaza, a blazing hot dusty arena, magic was in being. Hundreds of participants, men, women, and children, costumed

superbly as one should be when addressing the gods, were dancing to the chant and drum beat of a chorus of elders standing in
the center of the huge formation. The solemn multitude moved
with a curious and mesomeric unanimity. There appeared a
prolonged and reiterative monotony to the ritual, whose basic
pattern was an alternating stamping of the feet, with an occasional suspension of the rhythmic pulse, one foot held off
the ground, a turn, a side to side emphasis of the beat with the
arms, the men holding in each hand a gourd rattle, the women
two branches of pine or spruce.

We, being interested in the mechanics and construction
of the dance, began to analyze the rhythmic structure of the
simple movements. We were baffled. Our musician, Maurice
Peress, Director of the Symphony Orchestra at Corpus Christi,
and I laughingly refused to accept defeat. This was a challenge.
We would get to the bottom of it. We counted, analyzed, kept
track of the musical bars and suspensions of rhythm and of the
basic dance patterns and their interruptions. We tried again
and again, for hours, while the dancers, baked in a sweat of
exertion and fervor, danced under the merciless sun, moving
as one, inscrutable, God-like, in perfect consonance with a
pulse, a phrasing, an architecture of infinite complexity and
subtlety known only to them. We failed completely to reduce
this invocation to our pragmatic terms and formulas.

The memory of that rain dance, and of Jóse and me trying in vain
to parse it out, remained with me as well. Our task was made all
the more difficult because paper and pencils, along with cameras,
were banned. There is, however, a sequel to the story. Later that

day, I brought our dilemma to the attention of Louis Ballard. He told me that the singers and drummers, "the chorus of elders," adjusted their song throughout the day according to the position of the sun on the horizon, and the dancers took their cues from this. Also, that every Indian youngster learns weaving patterns of varying complexity—for example to form a diamond, we can weave

> three spaces/1 white\three spaces
> two spaces/123 whites\two spaces
> one space/12345 whites\one space
> two spaces\123 whites/two spaces
> three spaces\1 white/three spaces

And these combinations are related to the dancing patterns. In a way I am sorry that I asked Ballard for an explanation. I far prefer Jóse Limón's conclusion:

> The countryside was cruelly parched. The sun was molten angry fire in the horizon. . . . The ritual at San Felipe had been a rain dance. There had been not a cloud in the sky for weeks, for months. The next day there was not rain, but a deluge. The streets of Sante Fe were flooded with water above the knees. Dance is potent magic.

Magic Feathers

In fall 1968 Louis Ballard led a workshop in traditional Indian song and dance for BIA teachers. He also composed two works for the project, a woodwind quintet that incorporates the Sioux "love," or "courting," flute, and a big orchestral work with narrator, "How the Duck Lost His Tail." This was featured on a tour of the reservations by the Phoenix Symphony that I conducted. The story, narrated by Ballard's daughter "in full tribal regalia," requires that the audience (and the orchestra players) learn in advance to sing the Creek Indian "Duck Dance Song," whereby we would invoke the gods to intercede on behalf of the duck who lost his tail feathers, at the appropriate moment in the story. Chandler Goetting played a movement of the Haydn Trumpet Concerto, and the concert closed with Stravinsky's *Firebird Suite,* inspired by a fairy tale about mystical feathers.

In appreciation for the success of the pilot project, Lee Udall invited my family and me for Shalako, a festival held on the Zuni reservation in western New Mexico each fall. Shalako is, among other things, a time for consecrating the new homes of recently married couples. We gathered outside a cluster of new homes in the cooling dusk, watching as huge, eight-foot-tall Kachina gods, "spirits of the life forces," came down from the distant mountains. Slowly they approached. They entered the houses and proceeded to bless them with the burying of magic feathers under the earthen floors while they sang a narrative history of their Zuni tribe. The men inside the elaborately wood-carved and costumed Kachinas had spent months of study in their kivas, sacred rooms, with the elders of the tribe, committing the music and text to memory. They sang through the night while we stood around eating mutton stew with hominy and fry bread, stamping our feet to ward off the bone-chilling cold.

I did a lot of searching during my Indian year. What does our Western music have in common with Indian music? The visit to Shalako helped me resolve this. It isn't in the notes or rhythms, it's what passed between me and my dad when he played his oud on Sunday mornings, between Armstrong and Lenny at Lewisohn Stadium, Duke and his band in the Rainbow Room, Dvorak and Burleigh on 17th Street. Music begins and ends with the joining of two souls, one of whom can be a Kachina god.

Stravinsky

Toward the end of my stint with the New York Philharmonic, Igor Stravinsky was feted with a special concert on his eightieth birthday. I don't remember if I even shook his hand. In 1967, the Corpus Christi Symphony had a big Stravinsky weekend; on Saturday afternoon we did a staging of *The Soldier's Tale,* along with excerpts from the *Rite of Spring* for an all-Stravinsky children's concert; on Monday evening I conducted my first performance of the complete *Rite of Spring.* The next morning, my ears still ringing with Stravinsky, I was off to Los Angeles to meet with Gordon Davidson about our forthcoming production of Bernstein's *Candide.* I arrived at his office in the middle of some commotion and Gordon sent me off to scout out the theater, Royce Auditorium, the pit, stage, et al.

There was an orchestral rehearsal in progress when I arrived, Stravinsky's *Persephone* as it turned out, the speaking part being played by Vera Zorina, in a long Grecian dress. Robert Craft was conducting. Sitting alone in the vast auditorium was a small man leaning on his cane.

Holy shit, it's Stravinsky! He was apparently sleeping, at least his eyes were closed, and I went over to him. "Maestro, Maestro, this is a miracle. I conducted my first performance of your *Rite of Spring* only last night, and here you are!"

He raised his head from his cane. "And where was this performance?"

"In Corpus Christi, Texas." He grinned. "Probably the first, and the last, performance of my *Rite of Spring* in Corpus Christi," and back down he went onto his cane.

"Maestro, Maestro," I would not let this opportunity slip away, "I received over three hundred *errata* from the publisher, three hundred corrections for the parts and score!"

"Ah yes, we have had this piece engraved many times. [pause] There are more *wrong* notes than *right* notes in my *Rite of Spring!*" And he dozed off again.

8

Opera and Music Theater

♪

*G*ordon Davidson and I began our work together when
he directed *The Barrier* at NYU. Starting in 1964 Gordon
directed three semi-staged operas with me in Corpus
Christi: *Carmen, La Bohème,* and *Così Fan Tutte.* We had permission from Bernstein to do a similar concert-staging of *Candide*
for the 1966–1967 season; but the Corpus Christi Symphony was
going through a down phase in the usual "feast or famine" cycle
that most small American orchestras experience. The prospective
Candide in Corpus was canceled, but Fate stepped in and more
than made up for our loss.

Gordon had been engaged to direct a summer season of plays
at UCLA. We went to Lenny for permission to do *Candide* in Los
Angeles instead of Texas. No sooner did he give us his blessing
than he blurted out, "Don't tell Uncle Lillian." Bernstein was refer-
ring to Lillian Hellman, who had withdrawn her libretto after the
first Broadway production of *Candide,* complaining that Voltaire,
on whose book the musical was based, had ended his philosophical
tome with an admonition to poor Candide to stop dreaming of a

perfectible world, that life is unpredictable and bad things happen. So "wear sensible shoes and tend to your garden." Bernstein's grand finale, a huge choral paean of hope, "Make Your Garden Grow" ... and grow and grow ... was for Hellman over the top, and defeated the moral message she had drawn.

Lenny was genuinely excited about the Los Angeles *Candide*. He presented us with his "Pandora's box," music that did not make it into the Broadway show. Perhaps some of it would help flesh out our "concert version," which is what the first LA *Candide* would officially be called, even though it was tacitly understood that Gordon intended to let the piece "evolve." There would be some dancing and a unit set.

It was a miraculous summer. Carroll O'Connor, for whom Archie Bunker was still in the future, played the three roles of Pangloss, Martin, and the Narrator—optimist, pessimist, and Voltaire himself. O'Connor and the stage designer, Peter Wexler, worked with Gordon on a new script based upon Voltaire. They tried to work around Hellman's book but inevitably a little slipped in, especially some left-leaning "in" jokes. Connie Wexler, Peter's wife, helped with the costumes.

"Pandora's box" contained several treasures, in particular the aria "Nothing More Than This," which would strengthen the role of Candide. He searches endlessly for a world of peace and harmony and for his childhood love, the beautiful and pure Cunegonde. (Like those of Pangloss and Candide, her name is word play on her true character, in this case, a "grand vagina.") When Candide finally realizes that he has been chasing a dream, his aria "Nothing More Than This" expresses his anger and bitterness.

Everyone was doing three jobs at once. I orchestrated and copied the new material myself, including "Nothing More Than This," and it has remained in the show ever since.

Lenny flew out a few days before the opening. I picked him up at the airport. He was dressed in a white linen suit. As we drove to the hotel, he reminisced about his Hollywood days working on the film score for *On the Waterfront*. He insisted on serving me my "last supper" before the dress rehearsal, putting on the room service waiter's apron and a Russian accent.

The first Los Angeles *Candide* was a big success. Planning for the Los Angeles Music Center was under way at the time and our *Candide* production played no small part in Gordon Davidson's appointment as the artistic director of its new resident drama company, the Center Theatre Group at the Mark Taper Forum. Gordon has since made an immense contribution to the American theater.

Gordon and I had become a conductor/director team. We found a stage language—a concert performance that evolves into a full staging at critical moments—that would carry us through to the world premiere of Bernstein's *Mass*.

Opera and Music Theater

For centuries the opera and music theater world has attracted an immense talent pool of directors, designers, and young singers looking for a chance to work their way up the ladder—to get on that stage and *become* Carmen or Orpheus for an evening, or to be backstage dressing or guiding these mythic figures, playing with life-sized dolls. There is no end to how far one can go to create a new world onstage. The wig, costume, and makeup people alone are ready to spend the entire budget on their transformations. And it is all driven by glorious music and gripping stories. Many, if not most, opera people sacrifice so-called normal life. Opera becomes their family and home. I may be an opera *voyeur,* a part-timer, but every time I do an opera or a music theater piece, and I have done close to fifty, I find myself drawn "into the bubble." My normal life stops and I do not reemerge until the final curtain comes down and the cast leaves for home.

One of my favorite opera memories is of the soprano Patricia Brooks, who built a solid career at City Opera in New York. I was auditioning sopranos for *La Bohème,* and as she sang Musetta's second act waltz aria to perfection, her agent handed me a slip of paper: "Pat's fee is $3,000." I blanched. It was half my budget. Patricia, who was watching this mini-drama, finished her aria and said, "Maestro, if you let me sing Mimi I'll do it for half!" She had sung Musetta umpteen times and longed to do Mimi. She then transformed herself from strong, loyal friend, to sickly, vulnerable heroine, and sang the fourth act deathbed scene, and I of course signed her up.

Our Corpus Christi production of *Porgy and Bess* in the spring of 1968 had what I can only call an extraordinary "anthem of hope," grafted onto the final curtain. And I came away from that experience believing that *Porgy and Bess* belongs as much to the black singer/actors who bring it to life as it does to its creators, the Heywards and the Gershwins.

We were fortunate to engage William Warfield to sing Porgy. He sang in several historic productions, including the 1952 revival with Leontyne Price as Bess that toured Europe and the Soviet Union, courtesy of the US State Department—it was the subject of Truman Capote's first book-length work of nonfiction, *The Muses Are Heard* (1956). Warfield helped me through those tricky spots known only to those who have done the role. At the performance I was suddenly made aware of an arcane underlife that had attached itself to the work. Another *Porgy* veteran, Irving Barnes, who sang the role of Jake the Fisherman, asked me if he could stop by Texas Southern University as he drove to Corpus Christi and meet with the choir that was to be the *Porgy* ensemble. He had "some pointers he would like to give them." I said, "Be my guest." I suspect it was what Barnes told them that inspired the choir to do something I shall never forget.

In the final scene Porgy tells the folks of Catfish Row that he is going to New York to find Bess. He begins to sing the closing song, "Oh Lawd, I'm on My Way," and the company answers, "I'm on My Way to a Heav'nly Lan'," a familiar sentiment for African Americans, a spiritual of faith and trust in God when faced with the impossible. In Corpus Christi the choir made it into a personal *Porgy and Bess* anthem. On the final "Oh Lawd," the sopranos hold a high B above the staff—not the most comfortable note—for five measures; meanwhile the rest of the cast sings "but you'll be there," the sopranos rejoin the others on the three final words, "to take my han'," again ending on that high B. At this point the whole cast is supposed to cut off, leaving the orchestra to play out the last bluesy phrase, which ends just as the curtains close. But in Corpus Christi, when the curtain reopened for bows, the chorus was still holding the final chord with the sopranos on high

B! The curtain closed and reopened. They were still holding the chord. I found myself crying. Later that night, as my family and I were leaving the cast party, the choir gathered around us and sang "Oh Lawd, I'm on My Way."

West Side Story: *Fired by Richard Rodgers*

In the spring of 1968 Lenny recommended me to conduct one of the first revivals of *West Side Story* on Broadway. A meeting with Richard Rodgers (president and producing director of the musical theater summer series at Lincoln Center) was scheduled in his offices on 57th Street and Madison to introduce me to Lee Theodore, Jerome Robbins's choice for stage director/choreographer. I was of course excited to meet Rodgers, the composer of so many classic Broadway musicals—and one of my forever favorite tunes, "My Funny Valentine." I also looked forward to working with Lee, founder of Jazz Ballet Theater, creator of the original tomboy role, Anybodys. I knew her brother, Eugene Becker, from the New York Philharmonic, where he was a member of the viola section.

The meeting with Rodgers was short and pleasant and Lee and I moved downstairs to a coffee shop to get to know one another better and talk about the show. I had never conducted the musical but knew much of the music intimately from having conducted several performances of the orchestral suite, *West Side Story Symphonic Dances*. This was Lee Theodore's directing debut. We were on an even footing. Or so I thought.

"What kind of name is Peress?" she asked. "My dad was born in Baghdad." Without letting me finish, she brightened up.

"We are going to push them into the sea!" "Who?" I asked. "The Israelis." "But, Lee, you're Jewish; I know your brother Gene." "Not any longer; I'm married to an Arab. He sells guns to the Palestinians—" It was my turn to interrupt. "Lee, my father was Jewish, as am I. This is a very disturbing conversation. Let's talk about *West Side Story*."

And so it began. She reiterated the well-known approach of her mentor Robbins, that during the rehearsal period and throughout the run, "No Jet will speak with a Shark! They will have separate dressing rooms." This was of course meant to heighten the antagonism they would display onstage. "And the ending is all wrong!" she continued. "In the final scene as they carry the body of Tony, I'm going to have one of the Sharks trip a Jet. Like in real life. These guys could never stop hating each other."

Who was this person?

I suggested she speak with the book writer about that—Arthur Laurent's modern reworking of the Romeo and Juliet story ended with a parable, a reconciliation, brought on by the death of Tony. It falls in line with every dramatic work of Bernstein's—the hoped-for happy ending. In the case of *West Side Story,* "There's a place for us, someday, somehow, somewhere." A philosophy I avidly believed in and still do. We exchanged telephone numbers and arranged to meet again when auditions began.

The romantic leading role of Tony, created by Larry Kert, is difficult to cast. We needed a great athletic dancer who scales wire mesh fences, a singer who is able to nail a high tenor B-flat in "Maria," and an actor who can convincingly play a tough gang leader. The Tony that Lee was drawn to had a passable baritone, but his voice split off at high tenor G. Transposition would not help; we needed *four* more notes. Nor did he have a falsetto we could massage through the body mike. Lee insisted that she would get him to sing the B-flat. And try she did, with sweet-talking and threats. But we never heard a B-flat, just a croak. I called Lenny for help, prefacing my report with the "throw them into the sea and guns for the Palestinians" story. "We need to cast a singer who can deliver the B-flat," I concluded. To my surprise, Bernstein suggested I change the note to a G, a solution that falls far short of the climax the moment calls for.

As I write forty-three years later, I realize that I was not getting the underlying message.

The rehearsals proceeded smoothly. Jets and Sharks sneaked conversations with one another as soon as they cleared the theater. Tenors in the ensemble smirked every time our Tony backed off from the B-flat. I had a scary adventure tracking down what turned out to be the last remaining copy of the full orchestra score of this American classic—buried in an abandoned desk in the basement of the Steinway building. The orchestra started rehearsing and they were excellent. We were ready for the big day, the bringing together of the singer-dancers and the band!

There was palpable excitement in the room. Voices and bodies stretched to match the immediacy and edge of the band. When we got to the "Mambo," Lee called out to stop, and proceeded to address and instruct the band directly. I don't recall exactly what about, energy and thrust perhaps, but I was seething. This was a breach of director ethics and inefficient to boot. I got in her face and reminded her, with undisguised anger in my voice, that this was *my* rehearsal. If she had any reservations about the music she should bring them to my attention directly and I would talk to the musicians, translate it into musical terms that will bring the desired effect, and address the appropriate players.

But truth be told, I was about to snap. I am six feet tall; Lee maybe reached five feet three in heels. We began again. And again Lee interrupted and started giving the band instructions. I called out, "Ladies and gentlemen, it's time for lunch."

As people were leaving, I grabbed Lee by the shoulders—she later said it was her neck—and unloosed my frustration. "You are undermining my authority. I have to live with this company and this band for the next two months. Please, let's do this right!" And I left for lunch at our nearby sublet apartment on Central Park West. I wasn't home ten minutes when the phone rang. It was Lenny. "What happened? I was told you had physically assaulted Lee Theodore and she is trying to bring in a lawyer?" Lee had obviously called Rodgers. I described the rehearsal, the terrific way it was going and the way she interrupted. Lenny then told me that he had similar problems with Jerome Robbins when they worked on the original show, that in a Broadway situation, the stage director, not the music director, was the boss. He would smooth things out. Stay cool.

We opened a few days later. It was a triumphant night. Lenny and Seiji Ozawa came backstage, all smiles, to congratulate me. Seiji lifted the flesh on the back of his hand with two fingers and said, "You have this music in your skin!" I was very happy. A few days later I turned the show over to my assistant and left for Chicago. I was doing a concert version of *Candide* at Grant Park with a new, narrated book by Sheldon Patinkin. I would be back in three days.

A telegram awaited me when I arrived at the hotel in Chicago. It was from Richard Rodgers, firing me with two weeks' salary for "erratic tempos" or some such. I threw up all night. The next morning I found the strength to go to the first rehearsal. *Lenny is flying out,* I thought. *He will fix this.*

"You don't need *West Side Story,*" said Lenny. "But I do," I said. "We've rented an apartment for the whole summer." "Don't worry. You were great. How is *Candide* going?" I'm sure he tried, but Lenny was unable to undo this. The story did not end there.

A few weeks later, Schuyler Chapin, who was then managing Bernstein's career, invited me to lunch—a fancy restaurant off Columbus Circle, poached salmon, fresh mayonnaise, four forks—you understand.

"We owe you an explanation." Schuyler began to explain that the three principal figures in this affair had very complicated and long-standing relationships; Rodgers had resisted doing a Bernstein musical under his auspices at Lincoln Center before Schuyler embarrassed him into doing *West Side Story,* and he was not happy; the Robbins/Bernstein tensions are legendary. "Something was bound to happen and you were caught in the middle. We have made sure this will not hurt you. And it will be explained away." Not to worry. Three months later, at Lincoln Center, I conducted for Bernstein's fiftieth birthday a gala *Candide* with Irra Petina as the Old Lady, Madeline Kahn as Cunegunde, and Alan Arkin as Pangloss. Schuyler and I remained friends.

There's no business like show business.

Divas

I was engaged by Richard Pearlman to conduct what turned out to be a star-crossed production of Puccini's *Manon Lescaut* at the Washington Opera. It was his debut as the new general director and Richard went all out. He convinced superstar soprano Teresa Stratas to learn the title role of the French courtesan Manon, and to appear in the nude in a film that was to be integrated into the production. Between acts three and four the scene shifts from France to the New World, and the orchestra plays a lovely five-minute Intermezzo to cover this transition. Richard came up with a novel idea: while the orchestra plays, the audience would watch the film—made months in advance—Stratas, the heroine, and her lover, tenor Harry Theyard, descend from a stagecoach and climb up the gangplank of a schooner headed for the "deserts" of New Orleans. Being a Zefferelli protégé, Richard had their period costumes and shoes made in Italy, well in advance of the filming. He also imported set painters from Spoleto, specialists in eighteenth-century interiors. They enter their stateroom, disrobe, and start to make love. As the music fades, the film goes to black. When the fourth act curtain rises, we see them, live, descending the gangplank. It was a daring *coup de theatre* and I rehearsed with the film several times to get the coordination just right.

Well our diva, Stratas, for reasons one can only guess at, got cold feet three nights before we opened; she checked out of her hotel and could not be reached. Columbia Artist Management had one soprano who knew the role of Manon, Raina Kabaivanska. Richard and I flew to New York to meet with her. She refused to sing for us, even to meet. We stood outside her hotel room door as she shouted, "Feyff tousand tollars," to our every question. Dick broke into a sweat. He hired her of course. Gone was the costume, the shoes, the film, not to mention his elaborate staging. It was a night at the opera.

Within the year the travail of *Manon* was redeemed by our next production, *La Bohème.* The young Madeline Kahn—before her Mel Brooks film career—making her hilarious and deeply touching operatic debut as Musetta, and the dashingly handsome Allen Titus—the future Celebrant in *Mass*—in his first Marcello, were typical of the terrific young voices Richard Pearlman snooped out from his West End Avenue opera-coach spies. Duke Ellington attended the final performance. It was a triumphant evening for Richard.

Mass

In early spring 1971, toward the end of my Corpus years, I was passing through Vienna on my way to Regensburg for a guest conducting stint. Lenny was conducting *Rosenkavalier* at the Vienna State Opera and I visited him at the Hotel Sacher, where he was staying in a suite that Mahler is said to have used. The sitting room was dominated by a huge Bösendorfer piano. On its rack was some manuscript paper. A double window looked out over Kartner Strasse and the opera house where, in the love-'em-and-leave-'em scenario that Vienna thrives on, Mahler triumphed and crashed. It was Passover eve, and while Lenny was on the phone in the next room trying to get me a place at the Israeli Consulate's seder table, I started quietly singing and playing from the manuscript. It was a song, "Thank You," about a tree, delicate and sad. "That's beautiful!" I said when he came back. He crossed his fingers on both hands, revealing a Lenny I had not yet known—afraid, unsure, curious about this thing he wrote, as if it had a life of its own. He said he didn't know if it was lovely as of yet. "We'll see. I'm writing a Mass ... for Kennedy."

Lenny completed composing this two-hour-long masterwork, and orchestrated most of it, in the next five months.

Once, in exasperation and confusion, one of us ventured the inevitable question: "What are three—four—nice Jewish boys doing, writing and working on a Mass?" Lenny took us through his own reasoning process: his search for an appropriate vehicle to inaugurate the new national arts center named after our first Catholic president; the universal appeal of the Mass, with its Roman, Greek, and Hebraic roots; and the possibilities it offered for dramatization. The choice, he said, seemed inevitable. He was comfortable with not being able to find an explanation for everything, he said; one must accept, on faith, that there are mysteries that cannot be understood.

Bernstein outlined his dramatic concept—like Kennedy, the Celebrant holds out hope for peace, and yet he is struck down by his own followers. Lenny painted a picture of the final scene: the ceremonial chant, *Dona nobis pacem,* grows into an orgiastic rock-blues. A pack of protesters corners the Celebrant, threatening and shouting, "Give us peace now, not later. Don't you know you were once our creator?" All of the implied walls—between the vernacular rock and blues bands and the symphonic wind and brass players, the street singers in blue jeans and the robed liturgical choir—are breached, and the stage is filled with a roiling mob.

The Celebrant shrieks, "Pa-a-cem" ("Peace"), and throws down the holy vessels. He is at once Christ being crucified and Moses smashing the tablets before the idolaters. The frenzied dancing, the blues shouting, the instrumental wailings, and the attacking protesters are stopped cold. All fall to the ground, petrified. They watch in horror as the Celebrant goes mad. He dances on the sacred altar, stripping himself of all the encrustations of power bestowed by his followers. In only his jeans and guitar strap, he goes to the rear of the stage and slams the door as he leaves, shouting, "Fuck you and your war!" Lenny envisioned the scene on opening night: "The cast spread about the stage, and the audience, Nixon and the entire Congress of the United States, left sitting there, abandoned, stunned. And that's how the piece ends."

I knee-jerked. "Lenny, you can't do that!" He only smiled. And for the next month I labored on *Mass* with blind faith, knowing no more of the story than what we had been told.

Bernstein began, almost grudgingly, to part with the final section of *Mass*, his "Secret Songs," which breathed a bereft, leaderless, and fractured community back into life. I later came to realize that this manipulation of the company was Bernstein's way of protecting his message of peace from the inevitable criticism of the pessimists of this world. And as we discovered, at the end of Fraction, the mad scene, the Celebrant makes a catatonic descent into the orchestra pit—no slamming of doors or flinging of curses at Congress—and the deep polychord (A major and C minor) that appears in various guises throughout the work fades ever so slowly into silence. Lenny implored me to hold the silence as long as I dared. "You'll know when."

A querulous lone flute breaks the silence. The flute's final note is picked up by a child soprano, who takes us back to the Celebrant's opening line: "Sing God a simple song. Lauda, Laudé," the first of the keening "Secret Songs," symbolizing the kiss of peace. The child passes the "kiss" in turn, to a bass baritone, thence to a woman. The cast joins, helping each other up one by one, two by two. Chains of "Lauda, Laudé" canons begin to form. Their rebirth gathers energy and power as the orchestra begins to filter in with long phrases. As the music peaks and subsides, bassoonist and dancer, French horn player and Street Chorister are massed together downstage before the audience, forming a rainbow of humanity. We hear the last "Lauda, Laudé" sung from one side of the rainbow by the Celebrant and echoed from the other by a child. The mantle has been passed. The cycle can now begin anew. Bernstein puts forth the hope that one of these voyages of faith will transport us to true peace and redemption.

All the elements of the production were first brought together at a dress rehearsal for an invited audience that included members of Congress. At the end of this first-ever *Mass* the members of the company, and many in the audience, were shattered, in tears. The sadness and sense of loss—for the Celebrant, for our lost innocence, for John Kennedy—was palpable. That night Ted Kennedy came down the aisle to the pit to thank us. He was deeply moved.

I have worked on six productions of this work (and counting), and every one has produced this emotional reaction. *Mass* proves to be greater than the sum of its parts. Because the elements are perforce assembled only for an actual performance, the cast itself has no idea how deeply they will be affected. A large part of the power of *Mass* comes because the audience witnesses those on-stage discovering their loss and confusion and giving themselves to the kiss of peace. Bernstein knew that this fragile moment must be lived, not rehearsed.

Francis Ford Coppola, Opera Director

Kurt Herbert Adler, feisty head of the San Francisco Opera, had the idea of teaming up Francis Ford Coppola and me to direct and conduct the American premiere of Gottfried von Einem's *The Visit of the Old Lady.* It was the spring of 1972, Coppola's first *Godfather* film had just startled the moviegoing public, and only six months earlier I premiered the Bernstein *Mass.*

Based on a play by the Swiss author Friedrich Dürrenmatt— the English version ran for seven months on Broadway as *The Visit,* starring "the Lunts," Alfred Lunt and Lynn Fontanne—this highly dramatic work juxtaposes the bittersweet passion of unrequited love with a mob-mad murder. The regal Regina Resnick would sing the title role. It was a big gig.

We rehearsed in an old printing factory. The amenities were minimal: a water cooler, a single coin phone, and old-fashioned washrooms around which the cast assembled during breaks. It was pitiful. On the second day of rehearsal Coppola drove his personal movie trailer into the loading dock. It had two phone lines he arranged to have hooked up; an espresso machine; a refrigerator stocked with provolone, sausage, and soft drinks; a wine rack with decent chianti; a shower; and a cot. Of course I had to confer with him during the breaks, and Francis invited me to make myself at home. My liberal stance was challenged by Coppola's dark, Mafia-informed worldview. He focused on the empty half of the glass, and assumed that most people are basically selfish and cruel. This approach matched Dürrenmatt's, and he was brilliantly unfeeling in his staging.

Act one opens with a locomotive clanging to a stop, hissing as it discharges live steam (some of which descended into the pit—oy!). The whole town is there to greet their native daughter, hopefully their savior, the now very wealthy Old Lady, who makes a grand entrance in an open chair litter carried by two huge black men. "Francis, why two black men … in Switzerland?" I asked. "For an effect; it gets everyone's attention." It certainly got mine. Act two finds the Old Lady and her former lover, now the mayor of the town, in a wooded glen, reliving their youthful love affair, a cruel mix of sweet memory and sadism—she has let it be known that her price for rescuing the town would be the mayor's life. Francis's staging of the mass-murder in Act three … well, you know.

Regina Resnick's voice was thrilling but no longer young. Adjustments were made with von Einem's blessing, oddly enough in her middle voice. She was a great actress, a celebrated Klytem-nestra, Mistress Quickly, and Carmen, one of those stars who "take stage." Her Old Lady, charming, seductive, furious, and cruel, carried the evening. Librettos with so gripping a story often propel a work even if the music is mundane. I found von Einem's many-voiced love music in the forest scene deeply moving and his orchestra a potent dramatic force. When we met in Vienna ten years later, he told me that our performances were his most cherished.

As Francis and I worked together on this complex and emotional work, bits of our souls were revealed to each other. I came to realize that in the end we were on the same side. Francis Coppola attacks man's inhumanity by exposing and replicating its cruelest acts. His Vietnam helicopter attack scene in *Apocalypse Now,* underscored by Samuel Barber's iconic "Adagio for Strings"—music at its most openly vulnerable—has to be among the most terrifying cinematic statements of our time.

There is no hiding when we direct or conduct. According to my dad, the Talmud says our authentic selves emerge when we get angry, drunk, or do business but I have to add, make love, or work together on a piece of art. I mourned for Francis and wrote him when I read he lost his son, cheered for his daughter's directorial triumphs, and I regularly buy his wines—he would not put his name on anything shoddy—rather than play vintage roulette.

One afternoon I was waiting for a cab to bring me back to my hotel. Francis came out of the rehearsal space and invited me to join his family in a stretch Mercedes parked nearby. He would drop me at my hotel. The car was fitted out with a fully stocked "giligin's bar," leather seating for six, a window between the chauffeur and us. Francis explained that he had made a bet with the producers of *The Godfather*—if sales went beyond a particular million dollar figure, they would buy him the most expensive limousine in the world. His wife saw that I was wide-eyed. "Don't be impressed; only six months ago I was afraid to pass a check at the supermarket."

I was obliged by contract to remain in San Francisco until the last performance of *The Visit of the Old Lady* in the unlikely event one of the other opera performances would have to be canceled, due to illness, for example, and our show could be substituted. I attended other productions and was sitting in the house box one evening at a performance of *Aida*. Kurt Herbert Adler was in the box as well. The second act ends with the grand triumphal march; stage trumpets blare and Radames, Aida, and Amneris parade, accompanied by elephants and slaves. All join in a tableau as the curtain descends. The San Francisco audience applauded wildly as the curtain rose to reveal the tableau pose when three or four slave "supers" ran to the front of the stage and unfurled a long white sheet: "Dykes and Fags, support Proposition 18." The applause stuttered, then rose in approval. The curtain came down just as one of the lead baritones started pushing the perpetrators off the stage. I turned to Kurt Herbert. "What are you going to do?" "Do?" he answered, as he was rushing for the door. "I'm going to call the *New York Times* and the *Chronicle*. We are far from sold out for the rest of our performances."

The Great Communicator and Close Reading

All through my time in Corpus I continued to work with Bernstein and my mentoring continued. I sat through several note-giving sessions with Bernstein in the 1970s when we did *Candide* and *Mass*. The musical issues were dispensed with quickly. He would spend most of the time on the text, pointing out muddy pronunciation, either sung or spoken, for nothing was more important to him. Every word must be clear and comprehensible. A single dropped syllable could break the narrative story line that he listened for and protected so intently. Toward this goal, Bernstein always asked his singers to add a short "oo" sound before a word that began with the silent consonant "w" (e.g., "*oo*where" and "*oo*when," not *air* and *enn*) and a short "ee" sound before words beginning with "y" ("*ee*you" and "*ee*yes," not *oo* and *ess*). I realize this penchant for "close reading" of the text was also how he conducted music, a fierce commitment for note-to-note, phrase-to-phrase clarity. Holding the audience in the grip of the musical line was paramount.

Bernstein told me he preferred the sound of a high baritone for his heroes, like the young Allen Titus as the Celebrant in *Mass* or Larry Kurt as Tony in *West Side Story*. He rightly believed that a baritone delivers text in the more intelligible, natural male range of the speaking voice, as compared with the more "manufactured" tenor voice, with one caveat—he looked for a baritone who could deliver a climactic high note in the tenor range, a high A (*Mass*), or B-flat (*West Side Story*)! In my view the singing of Alan Titus on the premiere recording of Bernstein's *Mass* is the finest example of sung American diction ca.1970, as coached by Bernstein himself.

If we hadn't met for a while I got into the habit of asking, "How is the new piece," or "How is 'the opera' doing?"—that pushy "Mama" thing of never enough. But when Bernstein complained to me that it took him months after a season of conducting before he could "get all the other composers' music out of my head and start composing my own," my heart went out to him and I felt foolish. How dare I prod a man who had given us so much.

Ellington's Queenie Pie

In the late fall of 1970, at Duke Ellington's insistence, I was engaged by Peter Herman Adler, director of the National Educational Television (NET) Opera Company, to help Duke prepare a piano-vocal score and eventually orchestrations for *Queenie Pie,* his "opera comique" for television. I did this periodically for the next three years, through the last summer of Ellington's life.

NET Opera had given Ellington a commission, and the requisite cash advance, after hearing him sing, play, and tell the story of *Queenie Pie* while sitting at the keyboard—the Duke at his most charming self. But the vocal score and script were slow in coming. Ellington was busy, on the road, keeping his orchestra working in a shrinking market. He was getting ready to focus his creative energies on the *Third Sacred Concert.* Perhaps he knew he was running out of time. My task was to bring Duke back to *Queenie Pie* and pry a score out of him.

I caught up with Ellington and the band in January 1971 while they were playing a two-week engagement at the Shamrock-Hilton Hotel in Houston, Texas. I arrived early in the afternoon and went up to his suite. The scene looked somewhat contrived, as if Duke had said, "Quick, get out the *Queenie Pie* setup." Betty McGettigan, his traveling companion and secretary, was typing away at the script. Duke was on the bed, surrounded with sheets of manuscript. He showed me where he stood with the score and handed me a half dozen or so parodies of television jingles he had composed about Queenie's beauty products (for Queenie was a highly successful businesswoman as well as a celebrated beauty queen). It was Ellington's idea to "interrupt" his TV opera with commercials and news bulletins about Queenie's life and times:

> If you are agreeable to the eye
> Of your favorite guy
> You can make him hit the sky …
> Just apply some Queenie Pie …
> And try, I mean, BUY.

It was late afternoon and Duke excused himself. "I have to go down to the Ballroom. We are rehearsing a new piece. Would you like to come?" When we got there the band was warming up, parts for the new work were handed out, and Duke started rehearsing the piece even though there was an empty seat, the second tenor chair, in the sax section. In a few moments the door opened and the missing tenor sax man tottered in, obviously high on something. "I love you, Duke. I'm here." "All right. Paul, just sit down and let's rehearse," said Duke. One of the sax players expressed disapproval by shuffling his chair away from that of his wayward colleague. Duke started the band again and after three or four minutes Paul rose from his seat, stopping the proceedings. "Duke, I love you. You are the greatest." This happened two more times before Duke announced, "Gentlemen, thank you. I'll see you all tonight," and he dismissed the band. I was perplexed. In the elevator going up to Duke's room I said to him, "How could you let a *tenor man* ruin your rehearsal?" Duke simply answered, "You don't understand, Maurice. Paul Gonsalves was meant to be a priest."

What I did not know at the time was how Gonsalves had made jazz history at the 1956 Newport Jazz Festival when, "to bridge the gap between 'Diminuendo in Blue' and 'Crescendo in Blue,' Duke had him take a long solo … egging him on through twenty-seven exciting choruses that almost caused a riot."[1]

Some critics say this well-publicized episode resulted in Ellington's having a major comeback. But that doesn't completely explain Ellington's enigmatic reply to my question.

Ellington respected genius, in Gonsalves's case, a God-given saintliness that came with flaws. Duke looked past several members of his band that "used" narcotics over the years. The need to get his new piece rehearsed that afternoon did not take precedence over the risk of having Gonsalves embarrass himself further. It was a family affair.

The Gonsalves incident simply underscores Ellington's unique respect for his musicians. He knew something it took me years to learn. *Players* and *Singers* bring the music to life; they have unique skills and want to sound good. So let them bring their talents—encourage your first oboist, for example, to take charge of the long solo that opens the Brahms Violin Concerto. Ellington chose musicians who could embellish or even add a running musical commentary to his music, as did Sydney Bechet when he was with the band. And to keep the groove positive he was prepared, in a most guilt-free and graceful manner, to give up a rehearsal or, as we will find out, a challenging French horn solo he composed.

Queenie Pie was produced twelve years after Duke's passing in the summer of 1986 by the Music Theater of Philadelphia. Duke's son and heir, Mercer, controlled the "points," the shares of any profits it would produce. The Music Theater had negotiated for several points. I had one. But the production was held up when Betty McGettigan claimed she had cowritten the book and demanded a share. Mercer disputed her claim and we were at a standstill. Lawyers were waiting in the wings.

When I heard about the problem, I reminded Mercer that during the two years I worked with Duke on *Queenie Pie* Betty McGettigan had been typing the script for Duke and maybe added an idea or two. But more important, did he know about her devotion to his father at the end? I told him I met Duke's former valet/assistant by chance after Duke passed, and I complained to him that Ellington's sister, Ruth, would not let me visit Duke in the hospital. "Yes," he told me, "Ruth controlled the goings and comings until the end. But Betty McGettigan got through—she came in after hours every night with a quart of vanilla ice cream and slipped into bed with him." Mercer immediately said, "She gets the point!" And *Queenie Pie* enjoyed a fine summer run in Philadelphia and moved on to the Kennedy Center.

Off the Podium

Conductors live lonely lives. For every hour in rehearsal or performance I spend days studying and preparing. As I absorb the ebbs and flows within and between the phrases, the movements, the entire work, I mark my scores and parts accordingly: little swellings to bring out a particular note or notes, countermanding dynamics for the stronger instruments lest critical lines be overwhelmed, a bowing sequence for the strings that delivers an up-bow where I must have a short or lifted note or one that brings them to the top half of the bow for delicate passages. I play through sections at the piano to get thorny patches into my ear; and only after knowing the score intimately, do I listen to a recording by an authoritative interpreter (Monteux for Stravinsky or Debussy, Szell for Mozart) and then only but once or twice. During my concert season I live in silence; current works are constantly running through my head, faster, slower (I invoke "the six words"), until I arrive at an interpretation I trust, and this, too, will be refined in rehearsal, and yet again from performance to performance, ad infinitum.

I like talking shop, tossing about ideas, with a few soloists and conductors and especially composers I respect. John Canarina and I have stayed in close touch all these years. His grasp of the repertoire is encyclopedic and I often run my programs past him. And in his droll way he offers correctives: "You are aware that two of the three works are in the same key?" or, "That program is over two hundred minutes long." I have gotten close to one extraordinary composer at Queens College, Bruce Saylor. I hear almost all his new works and he likewise comes to hear my concerts and we offer each other support and trustworthy critiques. Outside of the college Bruce is the go-to guy when there is little time but a driving need for a work of the highest quality: Ellington arrangements for string quartet and rhythm section for Jessye Norman, a processional for the pope's New York visit ordered up by St. Patrick's Cathedral, an amazing "Amazing Grace" for massed choirs to close my Lincoln Bicentennial concert at the Riverside Church. His masterful text settings, the marriage of words and musical phrase, are natural and kind to the ear, which is why it is in his operas that Bruce shines. And I have been lucky enough to conduct several of them.

I welcome news and visits from many of my former student conductors now working in the field. They ask core questions and share stories to which only those who live the conductor's lonely life can relate. I learn from these contacts, but it is from working with soloists that I grow the most.

As a music director in Texas and Kansas City I looked forward to the arrival of soloists, at the very least to catch up with the latest symphony gossip, but more for what I could learn and share when we made music together. Soloists—pianists, string players, and singers—have been my ongoing teachers, my richest resource into the arcane subtleties of music making. They, too, spend an immense amount of time perfecting a masterwork; they, too, are concerned with the minutia of phrasing and dynamics, and they have a direct line, through their teachers and mentors, to the musical ideas of past masters.

My collaboration with Alfred Brendel was a case in point. We were doing all five Beethoven piano concertos in two successive concerts, a feat that only a veteran soloist can undertake. During our discussions about the order of the concertos—how to divide them into two concerts—our personal sense of each of the five works emerged. Which ones were the best concert closers, openers? What about the order of keys? Are there any issues of stamina?[2]

But it was during our first rehearsal that Brendel taught me, and the Kansas City Philharmonic, about Beethoven's use of the *sfz* (*sforzando*) marking.

Like most musicians I thought *sfz* meant a "strong, sudden," harder accent than that indicated by a *forte* (*f*) marking. But Beethoven peppered his scores with both. In practice it was hard to distinguish the difference.

Invoking his Viennese musical heritage, Brendel asked us to make a quick crescendo whenever we saw *sfz*—to start the note not with the hammer blow we had been used to, but with a light touch and immediately swell the note, a "wow," a burst of energy *from within* rather than a "pow." We tried it and it sounded wonderful. But "How," I asked Brendel in front of the orchestra, "how does a piano, a percussive instrument, swell a note?" He told us he makes a slight almost imperceptible "lift" before an *sfz*. I have been applying the "wow" *sfz* nuance ever since in performances of Beethoven and his immediate predecessors with good effect, and teaching it to my students as well, always crediting Brendel as my guru.

*Photograph 1. Mass,
September 8, 1971;
Bernstein, my mother,
and me*

*Photograph 2. Mass, June 1972; me (profile), Alan Titus, Jacqueline Kennedy,
Bernstein, and Gordon Davidson*

Photograph 3. c. 1928; my mother Elsie (Peress)

Photograph 4. c. 1940; my father Henry M. Peress

Photograph 5. The Tyger family garden, Poland 1938, celebrating the betrothed on the right, my Aunt Lena and Uncle Sol Singer, about to leave for America. Back row, left to right: aunts and uncles; Alte, Ester-Fega, Mallye, Gerson, and Menasha. Grandparents Moshe and Miriam in the middle; front, Avram and Sura-rifka. All the rest perished in the holocaust.

Photograph 6. From the top of the Judson Church, June 1957, the Chamber Brass Players

Photograph 7. Me, John, and Seiji in front of Carnegie Hall, November 1961

Photograph 8. John Corigliano and me

Photograph 9. Mostly Morton Concert, April 1995; John Corigliano, Morton Gould, and me

Photograph 10. Beethoven portrait by Stieler, restored

Photograph 11. Me and my children; Paul, Lorca, and Anika

Photograph 12. Ellen Waldron Peress and me

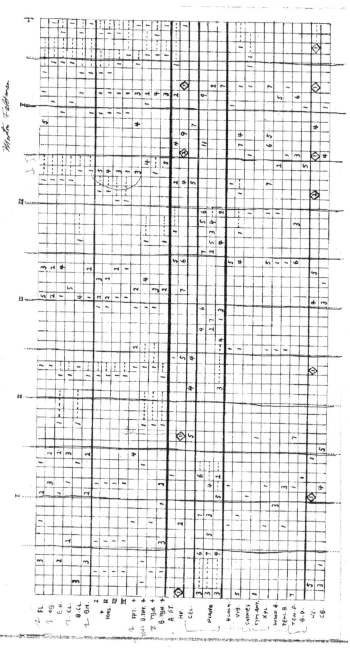

Photograph 13: Morton Feldman score page, "Out of Last Pieces"

9
Composers and New Music

♪

Although my abiding mission with my first orchestra in Corpus Christi was to learn the standard repertoire, after a few seasons I hungered for some new sounds, and I missed hanging out with composers. As a young conductor in New York I got a kick out of conducting pieces by my contemporaries, and often going over the music with them. I had this pleasure when I did Gunther Schuller's "Little Blue Devil" with the jazz legends, pianist Bill Evans and bassist Scott LaFaro; Howard Brofsky's "Horn Concertino" with soloist Daniel Cowen; David Amram's "Shakespearian Concerto"; and I spoke with Robert Kurka's very knowledgeable widow before I did his "Suite" from *The Good Soldier Schweik*. A concert without a new work, preferably a premiere, was rare. I decided that on my next trip to New York I would look for scores of new pieces. Fate intervened. I met Morton Feldman, in a snowstorm.

Abstract Expressionist Music: Morton Feldman

It was the winter of 1964. I was leaving for Corpus Christi after one of my annual New York recharges. A blizzard was on the way and my dad took me to the East Side Airlines Terminal, where I could get a bus out to Kennedy. He kissed me good-bye, not his usual way. It turned out to be our last time together. I can still feel the scratch of his beard on mine. The buses were delayed by the storm "for several hours" so I took a stroll through the drifts along Third Avenue, dropping in on some antique shops to warm up. I was examining some musical *tchotchke* when a roly-poly man with Coke-bottle glasses engaged me in conversation. It was the composer Morton Feldman. I had been visiting with some of the hot new music composers, and looked at new scores at various publishing houses, but nothing caught my fancy. Meeting Morty was Kismet.

We went to his nearby apartment to have a cup of tea and I left with an armload of his scores. By the time I landed in Corpus Christi I knew I had to play his music. Morty is not your typical American composer. I link him with Ives, Cage, and Antheil, composers who reexamined the very nature, the basic elements, of music: time, pitch, color, and silence, the absence of sound itself.

Feldman's music is mostly quiet, brooding and meditative, reflecting his friendships with Abstract Expressionist painters who were themselves wrestling with the very nature, the basic elements, of art. In Feldman's choral work "The Swallows of Salangan" there are no words, no bar lines or rhythms, only long strings of quarter notes to be sung on the syllable "Ah." All the singers and the instruments start together. They are invited to sing and play through their string of notes *a piacere,* each at their own pace, until they come to the end. By some flock-like instinct the various lines hold loosely together. If one voice gets too far ahead it is pulled back as if by gravity. The slowpokes are obliged to catch up. And magically everyone ends around the same time. The effect is quite beautiful. It took a bit of digging to discover that there was method in Feldman's title. The salangan, a bird species widespread in the eastern Pacific, "nests in caves where it uses its sense of echolocation, rare in birds, to navigate."

In Feldman's "Out of 'Last Pieces,'" the orchestra parts are on graph paper. (See photograph 6 of ms. score page.) The players follow their row of boxes; some contain numbers, some are blank. Each box is a slow beat of time. A blank box means rest, a number tells the player how many random high notes they are to play within that slot of time. There are but few dynamics. Like the paintings of Franz Kline and Mark Rothko that I saw hanging on the walls of Morty's spartan walkup apartment, there is color but no recognizable objects. Morty's music isn't about rhythm, harmony, or melody. Time, space, and instrumental color alone are defined. Clouds of sound float and bounce about, strong, weak, hurried, and slow. I played these pieces at a Young People's Concert in Corpus Christi, "From Chaos to Concrete: A Survey of the Newest Musical Styles."

The program started with a story piece, Richard Strauss's *Till Eulenspeigle's Merry Pranks,* then Webern's *Six Pieces,* Leuning-Ussachevsky's "Music for Tape Recorder and Strings," and closed with Feldman's "Out of 'Last Pieces'" and "Swallows of Salangan." The kids loved the Feldman as much as the Strauss. After the concert Morty ran around the auditorium turning up the seats. "My music got up the walls, and under the seats," where he pointed, "everywhere—not like the rest."

Morty stayed with us in Corpus Christi. He came directly from Houston, where he stayed with the super-rich Dominique and John de Menil. They commissioned him to write a piece for their yet-to-be-completed Rothko Chapel, a meditation center for all faiths. I did not know then, perhaps Morty didn't either, but he would invite me to conduct the premiere of his "Rothko Chapel" for the building's inauguration. Morty arrived in the late morning. I went into the kitchen to get him a cup of coffee and he followed me. "Could I ask a fayvah?" He spoke with a thick Noo Yawk accent. "Can I scramble some eggs? I've been eating all this fancy food done by the chef where I stayed in Houston and I just want a coupla scrambled eggs."

The premiere of "Rothko Chapel" was on a Sunday afternoon, April 10, 1972. I also had a dress rehearsal with my orchestra back in Corpus that evening. But that posed no difficulty for the de Menils. A private plane was hired to get me and my family from Corpus to Houston and back in time. I had been to Houston earlier that week for rehearsals and stayed with Morty at the de Menils' home, enjoying the chef's work and the fine wines. On the bathroom wall of my guest quarters hung a de Chirico, one of the bowler hat paintings that I had seen in art books. The de Menils were very down to earth and unpretentious, but I can't deny that I was in awe for three days. I just hadn't been in such close proximity with the ultra-rich before.

John de Menil walked us through the chapel in its last stages of completion: the walls reached up very high and were covered with a dusty wash—primer, I supposed. I was almost about to ask how soon the paintings would arrive when de Menil pointed at some transition and I realized we were looking at them! I turned my attention to what looked like a parachute hanging high above beneath a glass dome. He explained that it had been placed there after Rothko came down to see his work installed—thirteen huge and dark brooding panels set up in the octagonal space. Rothko complained that the panels, painted in the studio light of his New York studio, were being washed away by the bright Texas sun as it poured through the glass above. Philip Johnson, who had designed the building, objected to the intrusion of the parachute. A battle of artists' egos ensued and Johnson withdrew his name from the building.

The music for "Rothko Chapel," thirty minutes of slow, quiet, dissonant chords, sung by a wordless choir, seeped throughout the building and the paintings, "up the walls, and under the seats." Gongs and quiet timpani rumbles accompanied the chorus. Only the syllable "Ah" was sounded. The audience stood or sat on benches that were permanently installed around the chapel. The chorus faced inward with the three instrumentalists —percussion, harmonium, and viola—in front.[1] Morty's music reflected and enhanced the meditative mood of the chapel as well as the panels. A little more than halfway through, the viola, which had been mostly stroking long dispassionate licks, introduces a soaring melody right out of a Polish *shtetl*. I looked at Morty and he shrugged. "Why not? I'm Jewish. Rothko was Jewish."

We flew back to Corpus through a thunderstorm. I was never so scared but had to reassure the children and Gloria that there was nothing to worry about. We arrived late. It was a humbling experience to enter my auditorium and hear my orchestra sounding so good with no conductor waving his arms. Malcom Frager had started the rehearsal of Bartok's Third Piano Concerto without me.

My dad passed away that February. We had only just begun to get close. Morty and I met by chance, once again, in Venice. Years later after he, too, had died, I was back in Venice attending a violin recital in a venerable vaulted church chapel. The music filled every niche, caressed every column, and limned every arch. I thought of Morty.

Modern Jazz Quartet

My time with the MJQ was precious; we reached out to each other across the artificial classic/jazz divide. They get to play with a symphony, all those sweet strings; we get to be enveloped by jazz artistry. Their discipline all but shamed us: an incisive attention to time, its regularity and precision, and close listening to one another—only the finest of orchestras master that last nuance and refinement. Accompanying them taught me that my own time could become less than accurate and needed attending to.

As I write I realize why I include them among the composers I knew. Pianist-leader John Lewis and vibes player Milt Jackson composed pieces featured by the quartet, and John did all of the intricate arrangements, but improvisation is at the heart of their music. They composed a large portion of the works they play—together.

It was John Lewis's idea to model their format after classical chamber music groups; they wore concert attire and deported themselves accordingly, thus creating a serious listening atmosphere for their music. Their programs were not simply "sets" of tunes strung together, but rather John's highly developed, formally structured essays on bebop classics and American standards and of course, the blues. They remained together for over thirty years.

The MJQ played as featured artists in Corpus and Kansas City. Our last concert together was in Carnegie Hall with the KC Philharmonic on January 25, 1977. I also conducted for their RCA symphonic album, *In Memoriam,* named after the title of a work by John.

In rehearsals I noticed that the quartet's bassist, Percy Heath, and his fellow players in the orchestra's bass section were especially intrigued with one another. They huddled together to compare notes about bows and instruments—Percy had a fine Italian bass—and his infectious "walking" pizzicato technique. The versatile MJQ drummer, Connie Kay, was a master of slick brush work and collected an unusual assortment of mini-bells that he often used to keep solid time rather than the usual "ride" cymbal. I learned to lean on Percy and Connie's locked-together pulse, which I passed on to the orchestra.

The quartet and I were all in Kansas City in the spring of 1974 when the news came that Ellington had passed, and we found each other on one of the next planes to New York. We all wanted to be on time for the funeral that more than filled the Cathedral of St. John the Divine. Perhaps this is why I was able to coax them out of retirement for an Ellington Memorial concert in Carnegie Hall.

There are legendary tensions within chamber music ensembles. One friend of mine recounted how he had gone into a restaurant before attending a concert by the Budapest Quartet and the four members—two were brothers—were sitting at separate tables. In the MJQ the tension most people noted was between

Milt and John. John was an intellectual, knowledgeable about the classical repertoire as well as the jazz canon and a visiting professor at Harvard. His wife, Marianna, was a harpsichordist. They had a summer home in the south of France.

The "without whom" of the quartet, the brilliant vibraphonist, Milt "Bags" Jackson, was a legendary jazz improviser on a par with John Coltrane or Charlie Parker. He was immensely shy, a man of few words with a speech impediment and a lazy eye that I found charming. I so admired him that I sought him out during our performances, wanting some recognition that we were flying on a cloud together. Mostly, I got furtive one-eyed smiles as he spun out yet another magical flurry or laid down a perfectly placed final note at the end of his solo.

John was well aware of Milt's uniqueness and in many ways structured the quartet's repertoire to feature Milt's jazz genius in breakaway solos, fighting his way out of John's formal structures. On the planes between engagements they sat together and played cards; otherwise they seemed to go their separate ways. All this I learned from Percy who was the hip, outgoing jokester of the band. A former Tuskegee airman in World War II, Percy was in truth the steady catalyst that kept peace in the family.

Milt's Farewell

Milt—quiet, introspective Milt—surprised me with a warm backstage, dare I say, farewell, visit only a few months before he passed. I heard he had stomach cancer and was hospitalized. But he surprised me when I got back to my dressing room during intermission—it was a dress-rehearsal performance of *Black, Brown and Beige* in Teaneck, New Jersey, with John Faddis's Carnegie Hall Jazz Band—and there was Milt looking thin but with good color, and a smile, and in a sharp suit and tie. He told me he liked my performance. Then he said he was "okay health-wise" and about to start a series of gigs. But he stopped by especially to say thank you for all the music we made together. I was of course deeply touched. Milt Jackson was, after all, a man of infinite grace.

Alas, I have attended the four memorial services for my dear friends of the MJQ. I spoke at the last one, for Percy, "the Rock," as his brothers call him:

> The first to go was Connie Kay, the big tender *heartbeat* of the band. I remember well the three survivors gathered together at the pulpit. They seemed so lost ... it broke my heart ... and we all waited for the word, an explanation: "What did Connie mean to the quartet, his unique role, his art?" But the words never came. The best they could do was to squeeze out some platitudes or stand mutely before the casket. I thought to myself that what they felt could only be sung or played, never spoken. Then came Milt's memorial service in the Abyssinian Baptist Church, the "temple of the spirit." This time Percy found his voice. John walked up to the podium, squeezed his lips and held his breath, just like he did when deep into a solo, but couldn't bring himself to speak he was so overcome.
>
> John's memorial was at the Cathedral of St. John the Divine. I recall different folks climbing the high podium trying to sum up his life ... but in my view, they all fell short ... until came Percy.

He played some with a trio and when they finished he stepped to the microphone. "I'm not supposed to speak but I'm going to anyway." And this jokester of the quartet, the sly diplomat who, with a smile and a wink, kept the borders between John and Milt open and clear because he knew, as did they all, that despite the jazz imperative ... the defining grace of our American music that values the individual, even when joined in a common cause ... these four musical giants made art together in ways they never could alone. .... This quiet one, Percy, spoke with feeling and eloquence about John and the quartet's life together for thirty-seven years! Thirty-seven years!!!

Percy's memorial was the saddest, because it was the end not only of Percy's time with us, but of the *idea* of the quartet that he carried in his soul, in his playing with his beloved Heath brothers, and in his fertile memory. I had the privilege of hearing Percy as he showed films and talked about the MJQ at Lincoln Center. His grasp of their mission and their unique life together was masterful. I remember reporting this to his and my soul brother, *Doctor* Jimmy Heath: "Percy was deep." I begged Percy to write about the quartet: "This is important history and you tell it so well," but he demurred. "It's all up here," he said, "and in the music!"

"Americsan Salute": Morton Gould

Morton was a musician's musician, that rare composer who did not take him- or herself too seriously. Not unlike workaday composers of the past from Mozart to Dvorak, Morton was drawn to compose music to entertain as well as elevate, in his case music for radio, film, television, and Broadway as well as for the ballet and concert hall—as Ellington would say, "beyond category." This at a time when so many composers distanced themselves from the general public and, some would say, from the concertgoing public, retreating into the academy to produce absolute music, ever more theoretically based, eye candy for a handful of like-minded colleagues.[2]

A proper full biography of Morton is yet to be written, one that captures his humanity and genius. A work-for-hire biographer—who had never met one of the most entertaining, funny, and kind men I have ever known—began his tome with the premise that had there never been a Gershwin, Gould would have had a major career. He did.

I organized two "Mostly Morton" concerts for his seventieth and eightieth birthdays. For the latter I researched his lesser-known compositions and came across a Piano Concerto he composed for the WOR radio orchestra in 1938. I asked Morton if he would like us to play it. "You know, I have no memory of the piece, only *clusters*. I remember that I used *clusters*. Go ahead and play it, let's see." I engaged Randall Hodgkinson, a Boston-based pianist—winner of the first International American Music Competition sponsored by Carnegie Hall and the Rockefeller Foundation—and he agreed to learn it. As the concert approached, I asked Randall if he would come to New York and play the concerto for Morton and me. He and his equally talented wife, pianist Leslie Amper, came to accompany him.

"Morton, would you like a score?" I asked. "No, I'll just listen." Randall and Leslie played through the first movement and paused.

All eyes turned to Morton. He was straight faced, and we waited. "That guy Stravinsky's been stealing from me ever since I was a kid." They played the second movement, a blues. Again we all waited for Morton's reaction. "Shows you, I was as depressed in 1938 as I am today."

It was this self-unimportance that endeared him to fellow musicians. Indeed this very quality may have contributed to his success as president of the American Society of Composers, Authors, and Publishers (ASCAP) from 1986 to 1994. ASCAP was the beer-lubricated brainstorm of three successful but very different American musicians who met at Lüchow's Restaurant in 1914: John Philip Sousa, Victor Herbert, and Irving Berlin—March King, classical composer and songster extraordinaire. Morton would have fit right in, thus his being able to stave off an impending schism of the long-established bond between ASCAP's classical composers and pop songwriters.

He once told me about his first premiere, how he traveled across the country to hear Pierre Monteux conduct his piece with the San Francisco Symphony. After the concert he headed backstage and was just standing about when he was spotted by an apparently wise Mrs. Monteux, who asked him who was he looking for. "I'm the composer, Morton Gould." "Oh, please go right in. My husband would love to see you." Morton met the maestro and all but apologized, "Maestro, I want to thank you, I'm only a light music composer mostly for radio." Monteux then told him, "I, too, played light music, viola in a house of pleasure ... the best years of my life."

The "Mostly Morton" eightieth birthday concert ended with a takeoff for orchestra on "Happy Birthday" by John Corigliano, a longtime devotee who "owed Morton." As Morton tells the story, he was a guest conductor with the New York Philharmonic when John's father, the formidable concertmaster of the orchestra under Toscanini, Mitropoulos, and Bernstein, knocked on the door of his dressing room. "I was scared," Morton recalled. "Did I do something wrong?" John Corigliano Sr. tossed a few scores on the table. "My son thinks he's a composer," and left. The next day Morton called the concertmaster into his dressing room. "I have very bad news for you. Your son *is* a very fine composer!"

John Corigliano

Richard Pearlman introduced us. I of course knew his famous father as the intimidating concertmaster of the band during my time with the New York Philharmonic. John Jr. was then a struggling composer, earning some money as an assistant to Roger Englander, the television producer for Bernstein's Young People's Concerts. One of John's jobs was following the score being played, warning Roger when a particular camera shot was approaching—a close-up of a clarinet solo, or Lenny on the podium.

In my seventh season in Corpus, Jack Romann, artists' representative for the Baldwin piano company, called. A young composer he admired had written "a terrific Piano Concerto, just your kind of piece." It was John Corigliano.[3]

The next time I was in New York I met with John and his partner John Atkins, for whom the concerto had been written. They played the work for me and I was sold. I also liked John "Cee." He was a positive force, exciting to be with. Our energies matched. We did perform the piece; the two Johns would come to Corpus and live in our home for a week.

The concerto had already been premiered—not to John's satisfaction—in San Antonio, where John's father became concertmaster after retiring from the New York Philharmonic. San Antonio wanted a "name" pianist and Atkins was bypassed. This disappointment had left unfulfilled John's binding musical offering to Atkins.

Corigliano's music stands well apart from that of his contemporaries, in particular the academic crowd's fatal embrace of what I call the mathematics of the twelve-tone system. He identified, felt a kinship—gay and half Jewish didn't hurt—with the music of Copland and Bernstein. There are soaring tunes and lots of passion, dance rhythms and climaxes; his is my kind of music.

Our performance on November 17, 1970, was electrifying. John "Cee" played the Corpus Christi tape for his friends for years to come and I would like to think it helped advance his career. More importantly, we had made successful music together; for musicians this is a bond that does not go away. We stayed in touch.

Around 1977 John invited me to conduct at a new Summer Music Festival on the Greek island of Corfu. I was not prepared for the transformation of John's gay friends, and in particular the most musical of all tenors, Bobby White, who held their gayness in check until they got off the plane and immediately relaxed into their real selves. Dress, language, flirting, ironic jokes spilled over. I was the odd man out, the token straight (unless I changed my mind). But beyond the sheer entertainment, and pride in being included, I understood and was familiar with the veil that had been lifted. As a member of a minority I, too, once downplayed my Jewishness in mixed company.

On Corfu I worked with Emlyn Williams, British actor and author, who had long owned a house there and spoke Greek like a native. He narrated *Peter and the Wolf,* in Greek, for the local children.

Then there is the matter of the secret LP (acetate) recording I did for John. The story can now be told. His Dylan Thomas cycle contains a handsome piece, *Poem in October,* for tenor and chamber ensemble, to be conducted from the harpsichord. For the recording John could find no such talent and appealed to me to conduct it. He somehow convinced the harpsichordist to remain anonymous and, mea culpa, I am listed as "conducting from the harpsichord."

But this was not the end of the story. The other side of the LP was to be his "Oboe Concerto" featuring Umberto (Burt) Lucarelli, and I received an urgent call from John. "The slow movement of the Oboe Concerto is a mess; my recording cannot be released." The instrumentation was small, a kind of chamber piece between the outer movements, and John hired New York freelancers to rerecord the movement under his direction. "Could I come and help out? Please."

John picked me up at the airport the morning of the recording date. An ugly rain was in progress. We crowded into his Volkswagen Beetle and he handed me a score. There had not been time to mail one and this was well before the Internet and PDFs. I studied it as he drove and immediately saw the problem. To "give the players maximum freedom," John wrote the movement without measure lines; the players would each play from a score so they could follow one another. I now knew why the initial recording was a mess. I took out a pencil and started drawing in imaginary but highly practical bar lines. When we got to the studio, I went into the engineer's booth and John started conducting the piece. It of course collapsed several times, and time and money were flowing. I called out on the audio speaker, "John, please come in here for a moment." I said if he wouldn't mind, "I think I can solve this very quickly and easily; why don't we switch places?" This may very well have been what he had in mind all the time. I asked the players to take out their pencils and told them where to draw in my practical bar lines—not too many; I did want to honor John's concept while making it doable. We started again and I conducted where needed and, if I remember correctly, we did it in one take. This time I became anonymous. And my love and admiration for him is hereby documented for all time.

I was soon invited to conduct *Poem in October* in the impressively understated apartment of Miss Alice Tully, my old luncheon buddy and patroness of *The Barrier*. Sam Barber was there. We all sat for dinner afterwards in her twin, blue and pink, dining rooms. From our sky-high perch on Central Park South we could view the striking panorama of Manhattan as far north as the George Washington Bridge. I remember Barber quizzing Lucarelli about "good" notes on the oboe—I have since heard that he had compiled a list of good and bad notes for every instrument. Barber was composing a concerto for Harold Gomberg commissioned by the New York Philharmonic. Alas he died before he completed it. Lucarelli and I performed the Adagio from the uncompleted score in Brazil twenty years later.

When I was appointed music director of the Kansas City Philharmonic, I commissioned three fanfares for my opening concert from three friends: David Amram, John Lewis, and John Corigliano. We opened with Corigliano's brilliantly theatrical "Eclectic Fanfare." Brass players were scattered all over the auditorium, in and under the balcony and on the sides. A trombone choir sat onstage. I remained backstage as familiar brass calls started to be played; Beethoven's "Leonore call" to freedom by a solo trumpet, the Mahler "Resurrection" Symphony chorale by the trombones, Rossini's "Lone Ranger." When they all started to overlap, I entered, mounted the podium, and called for a drum roll to stop the cacophony; beautiful harmonies proceeded to fill every inch of the hall as I led the brasses in an inspired setting of Schubert's *"An die Musik."* Over the next-to-last chord a solo horn played Strauss's *Til Eulenspiegel* call, ending on a low pedal note, and we all sounded the tonic cadence.

When the time came to devise programs for the Kansas City Philharmonic's 1979 appearances in Carnegie Hall, Corigliano's name was on the rise. I believed, correctly, that a New York premiere of his piano concerto would draw the critics and an audience. I also honored Virgil Thomson with his charming and acerbic Symphony on a Hymn Tune. We posed in Virgil's apartment for a *New York Times* music section photo. Virgil chided John for wearing some kind of makeup. "I am too dark and don't like how my photographs come out." (See photograph 8.)

By this time John "Cee" and Atkins had separated so I was free to find a new pianist. Over John's protestations I chose Malcolm Frager. Malcolm was steady as a rock: he was totally secure rhythmically, he had a sparkling clean technique, and he had a name. John didn't think he had the requisite fire, but we proved him wrong. Carnegie Hall was well filled that night and the Kansas City Philharmonic did itself proud. Malcolm became a champion of John's concerto and scheduled it several more times in following seasons.

A decade and a half passed. On the second weekend in January 1992 John Corigliano Jr. owned Lincoln Center. His opera, *The Ghosts of Versailles,* was running at the Met (TV broadcast, too!); his *Aids* Symphony was being played by the Philharmonic; and he was being awarded the Grawemeyer composer of the year award, $150,000! That Saturday a party in the ASCAP atrium just across the street from the Lincoln Center honored John; it was packed with admirers. I caught John's eye, and all the hubbub and sound disappeared. "Maurice, would you believe this? You of all people know from where I've come."

For the "Mostly Morton" eightieth birthday concert at Queens College in 1993, John wrote a *festschrift,* a short orchestral gloss on "Happy Birthday." (See photograph 9.) Later that week I was shelving the score along with my other Corigliano scores and the Piano Concerto score fell out, revealing a twenty-four-year-old letter from John's father to me. It was sent after the Corpus Christi performance of the concerto that Corigliano Sr. had attended. It had not been easy for John's father to accept his son's being gay and there were strains. But this letter included a loving tribute: "You know that John junior has composed a violin sonata in my honor. It is a fine work and I am very proud of him." I of course sent it to my friend John Cee.[4]

The Dance, the White House, and Meeting Ellington

"I know, too fast, too slow!" Bernstein quipped when I told him I got a job as conductor with the Joffrey Ballet. Soon I learned that no one knows a score better than dancers. After hundreds of hours of rehearsals, of repeated listenings, every note and rhythm has been ingested into their bodies as well as their ears. This becomes especially apparent when a dancer sings or *ta-da-dums* some small detail from the piano reduction he or she had been rehearsing with for days, but cannot hear in the orchestra, something they literally *counted* on. I would often rebalance the band to accommodate them. As to the correct tempo, conductors who have good steady time and whose phrasings are natural and uncomplicated make dancers comfortable. The best ballet conductors spend time with the dancers and choreographers at rehearsals, internalizing their sense of the music. In performance they watch the stage as much or more than the score or the orchestra, and have a kinetic awareness of the body in space.

Mood also affects tempo, be it the communal spirit of a dance company on tour, or the zeitgeist of a nation. We approach the "Star Spangled Banner" differently at a time of national peril than when opening a football game. Choreographer/director Alvin Ailey on tour with his company in the late 1970s complained, perhaps for my sake, that even though they were "regrettably" using taped music, "the tempos still felt too fast or too slow from one evening to the next!" I thought to myself, "Had they been traveling with their conductor, the company's mood would have been reflected in the tempos of the music." The Joffrey Ballet got me to the White House.

Meeting Ellington: The
White House Festival of the Arts

For one jam-packed day, June 14, 1965, the White House was
transformed into a museum, sculpture court, theater, and concert stage. On the walls of the public rooms hung paintings by
Franz Kline, Ben Shawn, and Mark Rothko, among others; and
photographs by Stuart Eizenstat, Man Ray, Edward Steichen, and
Alfred Stieglitz. There were sculptures by Alexander Calder, Lou-
ise Nevelson, and Isamu Noguchi. Many of the artists themselves
were in attendance.

An event titled "Prose and Poetry," introduced by Mark Van
Doren, featured readings by Saul Bellow, Catherine Drinker
Bowen, and John Hersey. Robert Lowell, who declined to appear,
was outside leading a protest against the festival because it was
being held while the nation was in the grip of the war in Vietnam.
Set apart from jazz, a short afternoon concert of American music
given by the Louisville Orchestra and introduced by Marian An-
derson showcased instrumental pieces by Ned Rorem and Robert
Whitney and vocal works by Gershwin and Bernstein sung by
Roberta Peters. A program of drama followed, with scenes from
Tennessee Williams's *The Glass Menagerie* and Arthur Miller's
Death of a Salesman, introduced by Helen Hayes. Film clips from
Elia Kazan's *On the Waterfront* and Alfred Hitchcock's *North by
Northwest,* introduced by Charlton Heston, ended the daytime
presentations.

I recall the prevailing mood of that marathon day as stiff and
formal. The many luminaries appeared self-conscious, in awe of

one another. There were polite exchanges all around, little more. But that was about to change.

The evening's entertainment took place upon a stage erected on the White House lawn. Gene Kelly was the host.

Jazz was to be the culminating event for the entire festival, but first came American Dance. The Joffrey Ballet Company performed *Gamelan* to music of the same title by Lou Harrison, and *Sea Shadows* to the second movement of Ravel's Piano Concerto in G. Gilbert Kalish was the piano soloist. I conducted an orchestra recruited from members of the Marine band. Polite applause covered our exit; then Kelly introduced the Duke: "It's a long road from Congo Square to Carnegie Hall, and a longer musical way still. But jazz made it. Riding on the well-tailored coat tails of Duke Ellington some twenty-two years ago, he and the great artists of his ensemble took lady jazz out of her off-the-racks cotton dress and put her in a long velvet gown. Ladies and gentlemen, if there had never been a Duke Ellington, jazz would have had to invent him. And so it's with pride that I present the Duke."

A wall of applause rose in greeting as Ellington stomped out the tempo. The band kicked off with "Take the A Train," and the motley crowd of artists and poets, actors and dancers, politicians and glitterati melted into one. Ties were loosened, shoes and jackets came off. I remember smiles and dancing. We were caught up in the delicious, delirious embrace of Ellington's music. Ellington followed with "one of our latest compositions," selections from the *Far East Suite.* He then introduced portions of the featured work from the historic Carnegie Hall concert that Kelly referred to, "our tone parallel to the history of the Negro in

America, *Black, Brown and Beige*." I heard the work for the first time. The band still featured Ellington veterans Johnny Hodges, Ray Nance, Lawrence Brown, and Harry Carney. I was in orbit, carried along by the audience's obvious pleasure in Duke's music, in particular the haunting alto saxophone of Johnny Hodges, and the violin solos of Ray Nance, in "Come Sunday."

Having spent considerable time since that magical evening studying, scoring, and performing *Black, Brown and Beige,* I realize that Ellington chose to place his "tone parallel" alongside the other American masterworks performed and displayed at the festival, reaffirming his faith in the work, no matter its less-than-enthusiastic reception by most critics and fans when it was first presented.

After the Ellington Orchestra finished its set, Lady Bird Johnson, the real force behind the festival, thanked all the performers and artists and invited everyone to enjoy refreshments and view the art and sculpture on display. But the audience would not let the Duke and his orchestra go. The band remained onstage to play many of Ellington's celebrated compositions including, of course, the "Mood Indigo" and "Caravan" of my youth.

I was fired up, wondering how a symphony conductor like myself could take part in this important music, music that spoke to me as profoundly as any other, music that reached out and embraced everyone. Later that evening I met Ellington's collaborator, Billy Strayhorn, at a reception in the East Room. To my pleasant surprise, Strayhorn had heard of me as a conductor with some jazz in his soul. I asked him if Ellington or he had ever thought about scoring *Black, Brown and Beige* for symphony orchestra.

"Why don't you ask him yourself?" Strayhorn responded, and proceeded to introduce me to Duke. When I repeated the question, Duke countered, "What's wrong with it the way it is?" I explained how I loved his music and jazz and that I was now conducting my own symphony orchestra and wanted to play some of his bigger works. He was charming but had no more to offer.

I met Ellington again six weeks later, in July 1965, when he came to direct the New York Philharmonic in his *The Golden Broom and the Green Apple.* Here was the hero of the White House Festival of the Arts conducting his own music *for symphony orchestra!* This time, however, I found the experience disappointing. The orchestration was four-square. Jazz licks, and "oo-shoo-bee-doos" that any musician of my generation could scat with ease, blurred by awkward bowings. And despite having the master jazz drummer Louie Bellson at his side, Duke seemed uncharacteristically uncomfortable in front of the New York Philharmonic. (When I finally did a recording of the original *Black, Brown and Beige* "the way it is" with the Louie Bellson big band, Bellson was still telling the story of "playing a piece I never heard with Duke and the New York Phil, and there was no part for me!" Bellson of course knows that Ellington never wrote out drum parts, giving total freedom to his drummers to improvise their own. "This," Louie was saying, "went too far.")

The Golden Broom and the Green Apple, Ellington's tonal essay about an encounter between two women, one worldly wise and citified, the other a fresh naïf from the country, enjoyed no more than a lukewarm reception. I was frustrated for Ellington and for his music, with which I strongly identified.

I began planning a symphonic jazz program for the Corpus Christi Symphony with the Modern Jazz Quartet as guest artists for the 1967–1968 season. John Lewis had already composed several pieces for the quartet with orchestra. I invited Billy Strayhorn to compose a new orchestral work for the MJQ and orchestra for this concert as well, and he agreed. As the concert approached, I tried reaching him by phone (ca. February 1967) to see how the piece was coming and was given a forwarding number, at a hospital. I had no idea how sick he was when he apologized to me for not being able to finish the piece. "Blood Count," Strayhorn's commentary on his illness, which he composed in the hospital for the Ellington Orchestra, was to be his last work; as I write this memoir, I am having weekly blood counts; the numbers—indicating the progress of an illness—loom large.

Around the same time, I decided to tackle Ellington's *The Golden Broom and the Green Apple.* I felt it deserved far more symphonic justice than it received from the New York Philharmonic and decided to present it at one of the Corpus Christi Symphony's Young People's Concerts in the 1968–1969 season. In February 1970, I went to pick up the *The Golden Broom* score and parts at Ellington's library/office in an elegant townhouse on Riverside Drive near 106th Street (since designated Duke Ellington Boulevard). There I met Duke's sister, Ruth, who was running his publishing company.

With Ruth's help, I tracked down Duke and his band. They were doing a one-nighter at a college on Staten Island. I went backstage during intermission and announced myself as "the conductor who wants you to orchestrate *Black, Brown and Beige*;

we met at the White House and I have just performed your *Golden Broom*!" This last bit of information unlocked the door, and Duke invited me into his dressing room. He was wearing only a towel and a stocking cap.

Duke was, of course, interested in hearing how *The Golden Broom and the Green Apple* went over. I told him that I cleaned up the bowings and touched up the scoring in a few places, and that it had come off beautifully. "But why," I asked, "did you give such a high solo to the French horn? It's in nosebleed territory and might more easily be given to a saxophone." He was ready for the question. "Yes, it is very high but there is a way around it." I was all ears. "When I rehearsed the work in Cincinnati," Duke explained, "I told the orchestra that we would start the second section at measure seventeen, knowing that if the horn player had worked up the part, he'd raise his hand or come up to the podium during a break and ask me why I cut out his solo. On the other hand, if the part is too difficult, no one is embarrassed."

I never found out what happened in Cincinnati, but the notion that a musician's feelings could be more important than the music itself wasn't exactly in the symphonic tradition. The logic was Talmudic. I had found a new guru. There was so much to learn. Duke went on to explain that he did not want to introduce the saxophone into his symphonic works since the orchestra had so many wonderful colors of its own. The saxophone question would come up again, and sooner than I thought.

Ellington gave me a ride back to Manhattan. I sat next to the driver, baritone saxophonist Harry Carney, who had been in the band since the 1920s. Duke was in back with Joe Morgan, his publicity man. The conversation was light. I remember Duke's bantering with Joe about making such a big deal over his (Duke's) seventieth birthday: "No chick wants to share her favors with a seventy-year-old man." As I was getting out of the car on the corner of 66th and West End Avenue, Duke said, "You do it." "What?" I asked. "You orchestrate my *Black, Brown and Beige*."

About a week later, we met at Duke's apartment to discuss the orchestration. His trusted assistant Tom Whaley sat in. Whaley, who joined the Ellington organization in 1941, had recently taken over some of the scoring responsibilities that once were Strayhorn's. Ellington talked about the music. He told me the story behind the second section, "Come Sunday," about black people standing outside a white church they could not enter and harmonizing with the beautiful music they heard from within, realizing that they all shared the same God. He supplied me with a tape of the January 23, 1943, Carnegie Hall concert, an archival "location recording," and a set of full scores for *Black, Brown and Beige*, published in 1963 by Tempo Music, his own company. These were the only full scores (jazz band orchestrations) of his music that Ellington allowed to be published in his lifetime. Duke composed almost exclusively for his orchestra of handpicked players and, like most big band leaders, he guarded his scores from peering eyes. *Black, Brown and Beige* was the rare exception.

Duke suggested that I orchestrate the same three sections that I had heard the band play at the White House Festival of the Arts: "Work Song," "Come Sunday," and "Light." These three sections made up the original first movement, "Black." Our conversation turned to the scoring of "Come Sunday." Ellington balked at the idea of using alto saxophone for the haunting solo that brings "Come Sunday" to a close. This time his reasoning had nothing to do with using the available symphonic colors. Duke did not want "to tempt anyone" into imitating the extraordinary original performance of the alto saxophonist Johnny Hodges. Hodges had an uncommon, bluesy, conversational way of bending and sliding through a melody, reaching the true center of a pitch only at the resting point of a principal note or phrase. If Hodges ever left the band, Duke told me, he would assign the solo to an instrument other than the alto saxophone, in order to encourage a new and fresh interpretation.

We met again a few weeks later when Duke attended a performance of *La Bohème* that I was conducting for the Washington Opera Society. The superb cast included Alan Titus as Marcello and the soon-to-be movie star Madeline Kahn, who all but stole the show with her comical interpretation of Musetta. At the after-performance reception Ellington was the center of attention. When it came time to leave, I was still keyed up by the performance. The evening was young as well for Duke. We ended up in the apartment of Barbara Kheen, a friend of his who was a ballet consultant for the National Endowment of the Arts. High on Puccini and wine, we talked through the night. I felt the evening brought me and the Duke closer together. My later work with Ellington on *Queenie Pie* had its roots in that *La Bohème* night.

While my orchestration of a "Suite from *Black, Brown and Beige*" was still in the planning stages, an engagement to conduct the Chicago Symphony at the Ravinia Festival in July 1970 came through. The festival management welcomed the idea of an Ellington premiere (my new orchestration) on a program that would include music by Bernstein, Copland, and Gershwin. With this deadline now staring me in the face, I was bound to finish the score.

The Chicago Symphony Orchestra played the new orchestration amazingly well. My trumpet-playing days were not that far behind me and I was particularly aware of how stylishly the orchestra's legendary principal trumpeter, Adolph Herseth, led the brass section, swinging the phrases and working away with his plunger mute in the final measures of "Light."[5]

Ellington listened to a private taping of the Ravinia performance and, I am happy to report, approved of my orchestration, including my using the alto saxophone in "Come Sunday." His one caveat, drilled into my memory: "Take a more deliberate tempo, especially for the opening of 'Work Song.'" I have respected that advice ever since.

Not long after, Duke called upon me to work on *The River,* and more significantly, *Queenie Pie.* I became one of Duke's "symphony men."

10

A Music Director in Texas II

World War II ended in 1945, but it took fifteen years before the New York Philharmonic broke the ice and played in Berlin. Bernstein explained to the audience, in German, that it was Rosh Hashanah eve (October 22, 1960), and began the concert with a prayer for world peace in Hebrew! The Berlin Philharmonic, under Von Karajan, was first welcomed to Carnegie Hall, and America, a year later during my time with the Philharmonic. John, Seiji, and I lay hidden on the floor of a box for the "closed" and very brief acoustic rehearsal; and I watched in awe that evening as Karajan came out of his limousine and walked directly onto the stage where his orchestra awaited.

My family and I were invited to spend June and July 1969 in Freiburg, Germany, a lovely university town surrounded by mountains. I would work with American singers and a German orchestra in a production of Purcell's *Dido and Aeneus.* As for so many other Jewish musicians of my generation, Germany was off limits, along with Carl Orff and Volkswagens.

I grappled with my decision. At the time I was steeping myself in the music of Mozart, Haydn, Beethoven, and Brahms. I asked myself, "How can I hate an entire nation? Isn't that what the Nazis did to my people?" I had to eradicate this prejudice in me. I would meet young German musicians my age who had nothing to do with the war, or the Holocaust. I accepted and started studying the language.

The Austin Symphony, 1970–1973

After the seventh season in Corpus (1968) we moved back to New York. The pep talk I got from Kurt Weinhold of Columbia Artists, "Go down there and build a better orchestra and we will move you up!" was a canard. I was growing as a musician but career-wise I felt forgotten. We sublet a lovely apartment on Central Park West and enrolled the kids in good private schools. I commuted to Corpus for my concerts. I had other work in New York with Ellington and Joffrey.

A year after we settled back in New York, the chairman of the University of Texas music department came to visit us. He was authorized to offer me the music directorship of the Austin Symphony and a professorship at UT, as director of the college orchestra and teacher of their advanced conductors. I would have three orchestras and three salaries! "In for a penny, in for a pound," it was an offer I could not refuse. We would have to move back to our house in Corpus at the end of summer.

Austin in 1970 was very different from Corpus: no sleepy palms, no bay front on the Gulf, no Tex-Mex presence, fewer oilmen. It was a state capital where politicians reigned, and its largest enterprise, the University of Texas—hook 'em horns— dominated the cultural life of the community. After Michael Dell dropped out of UT in 1984 and started his computer company, Austin began to change. Today Dell, Inc., is the largest employer in central Texas. Music plays a large role in Austin's thriving nightlife and is central to its having become home to some of the most popular festivals in the country.

When I was rehearsing or performing in Austin—I usually flew up from Corpus—I stayed in a small cottage on a privately owned nature preserve right in the center of town. I am embarrassed to say I have forgotten the name of the couple who made this possible, but like other oil-rich "folks" I met in Texas, they were curious about, and supportive of, the environment and the arts. I felt blessed to be studying Beethoven, sitting near fragrant wildflowers, while bees and unusual birds hummed and chirped about. My biggest challenge as leader of three orchestras near one another was repertoire, carrying two or three programs in my head at the same time.

Lyndon Baines Johnson Presidential Library Inaugural

The Austin Symphony was invited to play a concert for the inaugural celebration of the Lyndon B. Johnson Presidential Library on May 22, 1971. Gloria and I were invited to attend the morning's opening ceremony. To get to the viewing stand, we drove through three cordons—Austin police, the Texas Rangers, and UT campus police. Instant lawn had been installed overnight on what had been a dusty worksite in the middle of the University of Texas campus. We sat waiting among the dignitaries and were thrilled to see Doctor Seuss among them. "What is he doing here?" we asked ourselves. Helicopters swooped in. We later assumed they carried General Westmoreland and President Nixon.

The tight security was to prevent protesting students from getting too close. The students anticipated this and must have stayed up all night to prepare a dramatic statement about the ongoing war in Vietnam. When the ceremonies began, they launched their protest. As the band played "Hail to the Chief" and Billy Graham followed with the invocation, thousands of black balloons rose in the distance, drawing everyone's attention skyward as they slowly, accusingly, floated overhead. Far away chants of "Fuck your war!" competed with the opening speakers. It was surreal.

That afternoon I led the Austin Symphony through passionate performances of American works by "my guys," Ellington, Gould, and Bernstein. We engaged Betty Allen to sing Copland's settings of American folk songs. At the after-concert reception Gloria and I sat with the symphony president and her husband. They shared with us that they "slept with a loaded pistol next to their bed" and at the same time they wondered aloud why I engaged a "Negra" to sing for the Johnson Library celebration.

"Because she is a marvelous singer, a favorite of Copland's."

Betty Allen was the mezzo in my life. She sang Brangene for me in *Tristan and Isolde,* and was my mezzo-soprano soloist for Beethoven's Ninth, the Verdi *Requiem,* and Mahler's *Das Lied von der Erde.* Betty was an amazing linguist, great friend and a favored singer of Virgil Thompson, and smart as hell. Orphaned at twelve, she made her way alone: "I scrubbed floors." Betty discovered she had this amazingly huge voice, dark with rich overtones topped with ping. And her voice and her brains got her scholarships to excellent music schools. I met her during my Philharmonic year. I remember how, at the recording of Bach's St. Matthew Passion, her rich voice overloaded the mikes and she was asked to step way back. Betty had a grand career as a recitalist and oratorio singer. She sang major operatic roles, mostly in concert.[1]

Alas, her desire to sing at the Met was not rewarded but, as I have discovered in my own career, giving back is far more important than adding another line to an already overstuffed CV. Betty started teaching and took over the directorship of the Harlem School of the Arts. At the same time she gave up her Upper West Side brownstone and moved to Strivers' Row in Harlem. Boards jostled to seat her: Chamber Music Society of Lincoln Center, the National Foundation for the Advancement of the Arts, and Carnegie Hall, where her recommendation sealed the deal for my Jazz Legacy Series! Betty brought her best students to sing at the Century Club every year; it got them patrons and helped the school. (I escorted her there for her last-ever monthly meeting.) How lucky am I to have worked with so fine an artist and bighearted human being?

That is why I asked Betty Allen to sing for the LBJ Library inaugural.

That fall I did the *Mass* at the Kennedy Center, Austin renamed their biggest downtown thoroughfare "Maurice Peress Avenue" for a month. I still have one of the lamppost signs hanging in my kitchen. At that time, Gloria and I were greeted at the Corpus airport by a big, white, open convertible that carried us at the head of a homecoming parade, a high school band with scantily clad twirlers up front.

I look back on my time in Corpus and Austin with a smile in my heart. Texans rightly felt unique: "You know, Mawreece, we could secede," said Van Cliburn about some political issue when I worked with him again. By this time I was in Kansas City.

Goin' to Kansas City

During my Corpus/Austin period I was a guest conductor with the Kansas City Philharmonic on two occasions. I was particularly flattered to be invited by George Mester, their newly appointed music director, whom I knew in New York in the late 1950s and held in high regard. At the opening rehearsal for my first KC engagement I found the band lethargic and lazy, and tore into them, woke them up, as I struggled to extract the poetry and brilliance called for in the Shostakovich Fifth. They responded and produced an excellent concert. Besides, I had nothing to lose. I wasn't auditioning to be their new conductor; George had just been hired. For my second appearance I scheduled Bartok's challenging Concerto for Orchestra. Knowing this time what they were capable of, I went for broke; I cleaned and polished and cajoled. And we did Bartok proud.

Then came my LBJ Library concert back in Austin. Kansas City's first trumpeter, Steve Weger, was hired as an extra player and he saw me in action with American repertoire, Bernstein, Ellington, and Copland. It was Steve who called a few months later to say that the Kansas City players were impressed with me and asked if I would accept an invitation to be their music director. "On my knees," said I, "but what's going on with George Mester?" "We forced him out and the board says no respectable conductor will now come to Kansas City." "Well, I am sorry about George but nevertheless interested. Your board will have to contact my manager directly." Things fell into place, I flew up to Kansas City for an interview, and they offered me a three-year contract.

I was *goin' to Kansas City.* I would finally have a major orchestra! This whole episode taught me that putting music first, getting a band to play at their best, gained true respect.

Between Corpus, Austin, and the University of Texas I had been performing twenty concerts a season; Kansas City played over one hundred. I would conduct more than half. More importantly, the Kansas City band could read through almost any standard work at the first rehearsal, leaving me two or three more rehearsals to polish and make Art. Before Kansas City I was more a maestro, Italian for teacher, a teacher for myself as well as the orchestras I led. In Kansas City I would be a colleague. We were well matched. In the orchestra were artists equal to where I was at the time. I would discover there were one or two who were more experienced, and I could, and did, learn from them. I can think in particular of the concertmaster Mark Gottlieb, born and trained in Leipzig, a second-generation concert violinist who led a distinguished string quartet for decades before he joined the orchestra.

There was much to do. I would have to give up my posts in Austin and the University of Texas and start phasing out of

Corpus. I started planning my programs for Kansas City. Within a week of signing my contract I contacted Aaron Copland and Virgil Thomson and invited them to guest conduct in Kansas City. Copland was an old if deferential friend. Virgil would become a friend and treasured wise man. I was privileged to attend his ninetieth birthday celebration. At the climax of the evening he rose to thank us and volunteer sage advice: "I have often been asked," Virgil began, "to what I owe my longevity and career. The only lesson I can offer is ... never to look back upon roads not taken. The roads you did take, they are the story of your life."[2]

II

Kansas City
The Roads Taken

*V*irgil Thomson's early years were spent in Kansas City and although I had but passing acquaintance with his music at the time, I thought that bringing a celebrated composer and literary hero back home would make for good programming and spark a broader than usual interest in the city's fine but beleaguered orchestra. Virgil begged off actually conducting because of a hearing problem, but agreed to give lectures and attend the performances. During that first phone call he warned me about Kansas City: "Don't plan to stay too long. It's a quarrelsome town, where North meets South, East meets West, Black meets White. The Civil War tore it in half and the bankers, who are always feuding, don't trust music. They like paintings, something tangible, with a price tag attached." Prophetic words in the least.

Thomson's visit was eminently successful. It almost provoked an NAACP picket line to protest a William Blake poem he had set, "The Little Black Boy," with the key line, "I am black, but O! my soul is white." This got us the attention of the black community that was well out of the symphony loop, and perhaps their respect, when Virgil suggested changes for the offending text.

To my surprise the music department at the University of Missouri at Kansas City, by tradition a competitor of the Kansas City Philharmonic for cultural dollars and prestige, rolled out the welcome carpet and organized a Virgil Thomson conference. And best of all, I found myself admiring and enjoying Thomson's music: the natural text settings, the charming Americanisms— church hymns, marches, and ragtime licks—his clean organ-like orchestration.

Virgil brought me luck. While he was still in Kansas City, the Chicago Symphony found itself with an ailing conductor and called upon me to jump in. There would be time for only one rehearsal of what was for the most part a fairly standard program of Rossini and Beethoven, the exception being the world premiere of Benjamin Lees's *Etudes* for piano and orchestra with James Dick as piano soloist. The Lees score, which arrived via overnight air express, was filled with complex mixed rhythms—3/8 followed by 2/4 followed by 5/8. No wonder the conductor had a bad back. John Edwards, the manager of the Chicago Symphony, seemed happy to let me replace the Rossini overture with Virgil's Symphony on a Hymn Tune, and then proceeded to borrow a bit more of the Kansas City Philharmonic's adroit programming, by luring Virgil to Chicago to participate in preconcert "talks."

Plugging in *Etudes* took every spare moment. Meanwhile there was one more Thomson concert left to do in Kansas City. I would still be learning *Etudes* on the plane ride to Chicago, where Virgil's fame preceded him. With only a day's advanced notice, the Chicago press and literary folks took due note of Thomson's forthcoming presence as much as if not more than the pending premiere of a new work or my last-minute substitution as conductor.

If I were to follow my usual instincts I would now be agonizing over the road *not* taken. Why, I have asked myself, did my manager, Ann Colbert, not take advantage of the situation to get John Edwards, general manager of the Chicago Symphony Orchestra, to commit to a future reengagement for me—"If you trust my conductor to deliver a challenging program he has to learn on the run with only one rehearsal, why not hear him in a program of his own choice with a normal schedule of rehearsals?" But "the story of my life"—thank you, Virgil—is that I did conduct this glorious orchestra and enjoy the man-of-the-hour high life of planes, limousines, a classy hotel, good Chicago restaurants, several thousands of dollars in fees, and an unforgettable elevator ride that spilled me onto the stage of Orchestra Hall. I hadn't checked my hair, shot my cuffs, fingered a "last arpeggio" on my zipper fly, or given a good-luck kiss to the gold cufflinks my grandmother had made for me in Baghdad, a habit I picked up watching Lenny kiss the cufflinks he got from "Koosy," when the door of a tiny two-man elevator that "takes Maestro up to the stage" parted, and I was greeted by bright lights, the immediacy of the band—I was still thinking notes and here were live bodies—and the sharp applause of the audience.

Virgil and I stayed in touch. We were an unlikely pair but we enjoyed each other's company. Thomson was a latter day Victorian esthete: openly gay, a conversational athlete, and worldly yet practical in a clearheaded, Midwestern, Harry Truman way. He was antidote to my natural big-city, ethnic, street-smart swagger. Perhaps I reminded him of another Jewish Maurice, the artist Maurice Grosser, a longtime companion from his Harvard and Paris days. He liked my wife, the poet and publisher, Gloria Vando, and later introduced me to the writer Christine Gratto.

I featured Virgil on two TV documentaries, played his Hymn Tune Symphony again when the Kansas City Philharmonic appeared in Carnegie Hall, and had him sit in a box at my reconstruction of the first *Rhapsody in Blue* concert, a concert he had witnessed in 1924. We had gossipy conversations: about the Gershwins ("They never part with a penny"), Lenny's *Candide* ("Everyone worked on it. It didn't help"), Boulez's avant guarde Rug Concerts ("If you let them sit on a rug, they'll listen to anything").

A memorial service for Virgil was held in the Cathedral of St. John the Divine on Saturday, November 25, 1989. I especially remember Betty Allen's rich mezzo echoing through the arches and her impeccable enunciation of an anonymous text, "Before Sleeping," from *Praises and Prayers,* as set by Virgil. Bill Warfield sang his "Pigeons in the Grass, Alas" from *Four Saints in Three Acts.* The Harvard Glee Club sang his "Cantantes Eamus," and Leonard Raver played an organ recessional, "Pange Lingua," also written by Virgil. I remember thinking the Gay/Straight, Jewish/Gentile, Left/Right, Harvard/City College, Paris/New York, Black/White, Words and Music generation, which so brilliantly illuminated the twenty years between the World Wars, and in whose lingering light my own generation still basked, was coming to an end. I hadn't yet realized the extent to which Virgil's comfortable pre-digital world of paper, pen, and ink; leisurely earthbound travel;

and ancient immutable political and ethnic passions was being replaced, overwhelmed. As I write, two and a half decades later, an ever-expanding wallow of music can be heard at the touch of a button on mountaintops or under the sea, without effort or cost. In the post-Virgil era, thanks to computers and their "garage band" programs, everyone is an instant composer, arranger, and conductor; sound, once digitized, can be sampled, infinitely manipulated, and reproduced by experts and amateurs alike. Virgil not only serves as my benchmark for the millennial divide, on the far side of which much of my own career falls; his sage advice has also helped me focus productively on the past, which helps make possible this memoir.

Build the Band

The Kansas City Philharmonic offered unlimited musical possibilities. I had access to top artists and could program any major work. But it also was a big business and supported well over ninety families with its annual budget of $5 million. The very conservative board expected to get their money's worth. The orchestra had been through several labor traumas before I arrived. I had lunch with my predecessor, George Mester, in July 2013 and we traded KC stories. He told me he had foolishly trusted the board's argument, "Make us a better orchestra and we will provide the money," and proceeded to fire marginal players, ensuing in the chaos that led to his early departure. Perhaps it was salutary that so filled was I with the excitement of gaining a major orchestra I looked past Virgil's warning and this unpromising history. I dove in to make my mark, but slowly the tensions resurfaced. The length of the players' contract was a sore point. The musicians pushed for thirty-five or more weeks—any less would not produce a modest living wage—while the board argued the city did not need so long a season. "Featherbedding," that word I'd only read about, was suddenly a real challenge.

"You have three weeks of rehearsals," said Howard Jarrett, executive director and general manager, when we first went over the season schedule. "There is no such thing; the band will shoot me; we need some concerts," I responded. After some arm twisting he got us a free outdoor concert in town, conducted by my assistant, thus saving my first appearance for the opening of the season. And for me he produced a concert at Leavenworth Penitentiary!

Having a huge orchestra with instruments enter a penitentiary is a chilling affair. As we went through three checkpoints, I viscerally felt my freedom being left behind in stages. I unveiled my jazz chops for the Leavenworth concert, including my Ellington orchestration of the "Suite from *Black Brown and Beige*." The prisoners listened eagerly. One, probably a counterfeiter, handed me a terrific quick sketch he did of our prettiest cellist. Another prisoner admonished me, "We get the best jazz players in the country. You should play Beethoven!" Yet another lesson learned.

The big challenge remained, getting worthy work for the orchestra, giving the board their "money's worth." Around the same time concertmaster Mark Gottlieb, whom I greatly respected, handed me a list, the same eleven players George Mester tried to let go. I did not open it and reminded him that I had recently gotten two quite terrific performances with the orchestra when I guest conducted and would in time make any personnel adjustments as I saw fit. We needed a period of peace.

Nevertheless, in my third season, the new contract negotiations came to a standstill and a five-week-long strike began just before the opening concert of the season. Itzhak Perlman was our soloist. In a never-to-be-published novel about a conductor's struggles in Kansas City, I aptly describe the genesis of the strike exactly as it happened:

> Board member Richard Stern felt he had a special relationship with many of the players—he was also the board chairman of the Kansas City Opera Company, which employed the orchestra every season. It was no secret that he was the person of last resort when a financial crunch loomed; he asked if he could attend the dress rehearsal and address the players. Our manager reluctantly agreed. He didn't much like grandstanding, there was too much at stake. I convinced our general manager and Stern that there should be some music making "before the talk."
>
> When I welcomed Itzhak onstage, the orchestra, trapped between their anger over the stalled contract negotiations and their long-conditioned respect for orchestral etiquette, applauded lightly. The comforts of habit and routine took over. We began rehearsing the Brahms Concerto.
>
> I allowed myself the naïve conceit that perhaps, just perhaps, Music, this music of the heart in particular, will unlock the impasse between the Board and the orchestra and make everyone aware of what they are in danger of losing. It was clear that most of the orchestra was thinking along the very same lines, for with inordinate skill and poetry the violins sang through

the simple chordal outline of the opening melody. They gently keened the hauntingly lyrical second theme and added urgency to the ascending phrase that ends the introduction in preparation for the soloist. All eyes and ears turned to Itzhak, who never thought twice about the treacherous opening octaves. He launched into the elaborate repetition of the exposition, this time redoubling the passion and warmth it received from the orchestra. The room was electrified, some were crying.

When the movement ended the band applauded Itzhak by rapping their bows on the backs of their fiddles and with the "silent" sliding of feet that players use to commend their colleagues after a difficult or well-phrased solo. Our personnel manager, Vince Bilardo, motioned me; general managers, Jarrett and Stern, have arrived. I left the podium, and with a heavy heart I carried Itzhak's fiddle as he slowly made his way off stage on crutches.

By now Itzhak realized that something portentous was in the air. Like most soloists, he floats miles above the bloodletting that plagues mid-level American orchestras. But he was about to be brought down to earth. The members of the orchestra sat on their chairs and stools, lifeless instruments at hand. Their faces were of stone. Not a sound could be heard.

I am well aware that the podium represents truth far more than power, and was not surprised by the sudden awkwardness of two highly sophisticated businessmen making their way to the podium. "This is no board room," I told myself. "They are in for a big surprise."

Jarrett was notably brief. "Good morning, ladies and gentlemen of the orchestra. You all know Richard Stern. He is very concerned about the current situation and has asked to speak to you."

Richard Stern appeared out of character, uncomfortable. It was his hands. They seemed at sea. Lighting up a Dunhill with his fancy gold lighter might have helped. Stern grimaced and launched in, "You all know why I am here. I have long supported you. And if you do not play tonight's concert I will have nothing to do with you ever again."

Stern waited. "Well?"

The band seemed struck dumb. The long silence was finally broken by Dale Weddel, the fourth horn player, a newly elected member of the Orchestra Committee, who slowly rose. "I beg your pardon, Mr. Stern, but you don't support me. I support me. I earn my salary playing horn in this orchestra. And I am not going to sit here and listen to threats." He started packing his instrument and others followed. Within moments almost all of the players seemed to be turning their backs on an angry and shocked Stern, who was trapped at the podium as they walked out.

Itzhak, who was watching the drama from backstage, turned to me. "What happens now?"

"I am afraid that there will be no concert tonight. We are on strike."

"No concert? On strike!"

He was apoplectic, in a state of disbelief. Then suddenly he realized that according to the Act of God clause in the contract, this meant no fee! Not even airfare or hotel. "I will never play in this damned city again!"

Itzhak Perlman went to his hotel to repack, and took the first plane available back to New York. I suggested to our manager it would be politic to at least pick up Perlman's hotel and travel costs but the idea was turned down. Of course over the next decade Perlman did play in Kansas City.

The symphony ladies were left with their hair all done up, new designer dresses waiting to be donned, and nowhere to go. The hosts of the after-concert reception went to some trouble sprucing up their Old Oaks mansion for the occasion, and now had no one to receive. The Symphony Guild president decided to donate the caterer's truckload of gourmet food "to the poor."

I was advised to follow the established protocol of sitting on the fence until the strike was over. I left town the very next day for Padre Island, where I would be safely out of the line of fire. In my briefcase I carried scores for the next six weeks' concerts. I would study them as if the concerts were still in progress, "for when we have a settlement and the season recommences." While I could not risk showing favoritism toward either side and must remain neutral, I nevertheless left my private phone number with the one member of the Orchestra Committee I could trust, "just in case."

On the fifth week of the strike Jarrett called to say that negotiations were reopened. He had surmised my guiding hand behind the Save the Orchestra Concert the musicians had organized "on their own," and he warned me once again to lay low and remain neutral. He wouldn't share the details of the board's new offer that was finally bringing the two sides together, just an enigmatic "you will be happy, if this works."

I returned to Kansas City, to be there in person as my Humpty Dumpty world was about to be put back together again. A few days later I got a phone call from Dale Weddle. "Maestro! The Orchestra Strike Committee would like to visit you, and right away."

When they arrived at my house they were obviously nervous but elated. "Maestro, we want you to be the first to know that the orchestra is going to accept management's latest offer. The strike is ended!"

I was shaking. I grabbed their hands with both of mine. Our first flutist pressed her lips together, stifling a scream. They were now relinquishing their power, not to the board, not to management, nor the press, but to their Maestro. Tacitly, they were saying, "Now it's your job to make sure the orchestra and music remain safe."

The painful irony remains that from the Symphony Board's perspective the financial settlement, a small raise, that ended the strike more than paid for itself. Pledges and contributions had not diminished and for five weeks there were no artist fees or health benefits to pay, nor the huge orchestra payroll to meet. Hardly any of the subscribers asked to be reimbursed for the missed concerts. The Orchestra Society emerged from the strike with the best balance sheet it had in years. And the final irony, that it would take six seasons before the salary increases won by the musicians would make up for their five weeks of lost income, can only be explained as the price paid for a psychological victory—an echo of the old class struggle in this new classless society. For when all was said and done, the orchestra players withheld their services as a public declaration of self-respect.

I blossomed in Kansas City despite this embittering strike in the middle of my tenure. I opened my first season prophetically with Mahler's Symphony #2, "Resurrection," preceded by three fanfares for the occasion—gifts from John Lewis, David Amram, and John Corigliano—and Stravinsky's curious but effective setting of the "Star Spangled Banner." During my six years I gave the board their money's worth, resolved featherbedding arguments, and was even able to replace a few weak players without bringing down the house. In addition to the symphonic subscription concerts in the Municipal Auditorium, I introduced a jazz/ classic series, "Mozart I Love You Madly," in an old theater set up like a cabaret. I did sit-on-the-floor "Apple Concerts" for college kids that began with my throwing apples into the crowd. The ever-popular "12th Street Rag" got its name from Kansas City's tenderloin district, and we opened with it on a television documentary, "Ragtime and the Concert Hall," featuring interviews with Eubie Blake, Virgil Thomson, and Charlie Parker's clarinet teacher, a "ragtimer." I brought the orchestra to the Kennedy Center and Carnegie Hall, and created two in-depth festivals: the first, in conjunction with the Nelson-Atkins Museum of Art, honored Beethoven, his music, and his world; the second celebrated Leonard Bernstein on his sixtieth birthday. Lenny attended.

Mass *in Kansas City*

In early May 1977, the Kansas City Philharmonic was presenting a full production of *Mass* in the magnificent Reformed Latter Day Saints Auditorium in Independence, Missouri. The coming together of all the elements of *Mass* produces an unusual emotional experience for the musicians, actors, singers, and dancers, who, after working independently for weeks on their own parts, would discover the piece as a whole only at the dress rehearsal. This may have been planned, in which case it was an act of immense genius on Bernstein's part. As conductor I was the heartbeat of the piece but I, too, was unprepared for the spiritual (the only word that encompasses what I felt) power of the work. This effect was evident in Cincinnati when the orchestra refused to parade and use lyres, a music bracket used by marching bands, but they changed their collective minds immediately after they experienced the first coming together of the piece with the choirs and soloists. And again in Reformed Latter Day Saints Auditorium in Independence, Missouri, the power of the work reached out.

I called Lenny. "You gotta see this! The building, a huge oval, seating six thousand, with a magnificent organ, was built for *Mass.*"

"I'm Coming Out!"

I often wonder if the very proper Helen Coates had remained as Lenny's trusted assistant, or if Schuyler Chapin was still Lenny's personal manager instead of Harry Kraut—would I have heard Lenny's sobering answer to my enthusiastic call:

"I'm coming out, what do you think?"

I took my time before responding. This was the first time Lenny opened up his private life to me. "Coming out" had become the Gay Liberation movement mantra.

Finally I answered, "Lenny, everyone knows. The gay world doesn't need your blessing. You have a family."

I did not know he had already moved out of the family home in the Dakota in late 1976 to live with Tom Cothran, a quiet and sweet young man. I met him five years earlier, during the final preparations of *Mass* in Washington, DC, when he was responsible for maintaining the "bible," keeping up with all the corrections and final versions in the vocal and complete scores that would go to the publishers. I was advising a dear friend not to separate from his wife and family.

If Meryle Secrest's timeline is accurate, my call was made when Lenny had just moved back to the Dakota, "a reconciliation with Felicia in April 1977," but he was obviously still conflicted when he heard from me, his loyal protégé in faraway Kansas City.[1]

Sad news followed. It pleased me that Lenny was back with Felicia when I heard that the breast cancer that she had been treated for in the mid-1970s showed up in her lungs in July 1977. She died at age fifty-six in June of 1978, the summer of Lenny's sixtieth birthday.

Washington's National Symphony Orchestra celebrated Lenny's exact birthday, August 25, with a gala outdoor afternoon concert at Wolf Trap National Park. I sat with Bill Schuman and Aaron Copland in a high box. We had been drinking wine; it may have prompted Bill to confide in me, "It was hard enough trying to make a career as a composer with the name Schuman, but to be born the same year as Leonard Bernstein?"

Lillian Hellman spoke from the stage. Her relationship with Lenny was complicated. I never forgot "Don't tell Uncle Lillian," Lenny's warning when he allowed me to do *Candide* for the first time. Hellman began by listing Lenny's accomplishments, then referred to the recent loss of Felicia, his anchor, and before all present Hellman ended her talk with a rabbinic proscription, something like, "We expect, no insist, that your work is far from finished," challenging Bernstein to take charge of himself and move on.

Kansas City Festivals

The Beethoven Festival took place over five days, April 28 to June 4, 1978. The orchestra presented three evening concerts: the opera *Fidelio,* Beethoven's first and last symphonies (the Ninth in the Mahler edition), and a re-creation of the December 1813 concert at which Beethoven introduced his Seventh Symphony along with his campy "Wellington's Victory" and marches by Dussek and Pleyel featuring Andreas Maelzel's mechanical trumpeter with orchestra—a costumed-mime trumpeter was wheeled onstage, I twisted a wind-up ratchet in his pocket, and an offstage synthesizer player sounded the tunes while I conducted the orchestra. For the battles in "Wellington's Victory" we split the audience into British and French, with hats, horns, and rattles, and they were invited to join the fray at the appropriate moments.

Ted Coe, director of the Nelson-Atkins Museum, happily joined our efforts and together we curated an "Art in the Time of Beethoven" exhibition. Audiences enjoyed daily chamber music programs surrounded by Empire furnishings, paintings, period instruments and concert billboards, an original "Peanuts" Beethoven cartoon, and three rare treasures: the now brilliantly colored Joseph Karl Stieler portrait of Beethoven, the only one done from life; the holograph of the "Spring Sonata" in Beethoven's own hand; and one recital featured an unrestored but functioning early nineteenth-century pianoforte (with a pedal-operated Turkish bell).

We were offering Kansas City a total immersion into the sounds and sights of Beethoven's Vienna. (See photograph 10 of the portrait.)[2]

The Leonard Bernstein Festival (May 4–7, 1979) honored his sixtieth birthday year. I had conducted a concert version of *Candide* at Lincoln Center for his fiftieth birthday. This time I wanted to cover the breadth of his musical output.

On Friday night, May 4, in the Hallmark Crown Center's intimate theater, a gala audience enjoyed the only time Leonard Bernstein performed in Kansas City. It came at the end of an evening of his chamber music. We were doing my arrangement of what I believe to be one of Bernstein's finest, yet rarely performed, scores, *Songfest: A Cycle of American Poems for Six Singers and Orchestra,* then his most recent work. Each of the singers sang a solo before joining forces for the finale, a setting of "Israfel" by Edgar Allan Poe. There I stopped and offered the baton to Lenny sitting in the audience—this was NOT planned—the applause urged him onto the stage and everyone, including me, was thrilled.

On Saturday afternoon my marvelous assistant, Frank Collura, conducted a dance matinee. We imported the American Ballet Theatre company for a performance of *Fancy Free,* and presented a new solo work by choreographer John Butler, for Judith Jamison, set to the "Three Meditations from *Mass,*" with solo cellist Paul Tobius and orchestra.

On Saturday evening we celebrated Bernstein's theater music. We showed a film clip of a frantic Madeline Kahn in Mel Brooks's *Young Frankenstein* when she looks down at the loins of the monster who is about to mount her. Fear turns to ecstasy, and she warbles, "Ah, sweet mystery of life." The clip ended and there was Madeline onstage, in the flesh, singing "What a Movie!" from Bernstein's *Trouble in Tahiti*—the trapped suburbanite housewife washing dishes and fantasizing herself a glamorous screen actress. This showstopping juxtaposition was the brainstorm of Jack Gottlieb, Bernstein's longtime assistant. There were songs of escape, and change, and hope, performed by Broadway stars Betty Comden and Adolph Green, Gwen Bradley, Madeline, and Larry Kert. The evening ended with the entire company, chorus, and orchestra singing the stirring finale, "Make Your Garden Grow," from *Candide*. On Tuesday night we performed Bernstein's three symphonies: *Jeremiah* mourns the tragedy of the Holocaust; *Age of Anxiety*, with Lucas Foss as featured solo pianist, expounds on the emptiness of modern life; and *Kaddish* implores the God we invented to save the world and mankind lest we forget him.

Aaron Copland

Aaron Copland came to conduct the Kansas City Philharmonic in 1975, during my third season. Aaron joined our family for dinner the night before his first rehearsal. He was totally charming, but told some of the same stories more than once. I was leaving town for another engagement and naturally being worried I alerted Mark Gottlieb, our concertmaster, to have an extra set of scores nearby. When I called the next day to check, Mark said that the rehearsal went without a hitch, that Copland was on top of the music in every way! Yet the memory issue surfaced again when we were preparing for the Bernstein festival. I called Aaron and asked if he would write a short birthday fanfare for Lenny, "ten bars" I urged. He declined, saying, "I haven't felt the muse to compose for some time now." Being a persistent cuss I called again and got his assistant. "Aaron is at the piano every day, writing music, but it's music he has already composed." Assuming from his earlier appearance with the Kansas City Philharmonic that his musical mind was intact, I would love to see those pages, to see what he added or refined.

In the 1960s, I did an ambitious educational TV concert with the Corpus Christi Symphony, à la Lenny, "Folk Music and the Concert Hall." It featured Copland's *El Salón México,* and Copland agreed to do an interview on camera. We met in New York in my mother-in-law's apartment on 57th street, directly across from Carnegie Hall. Copland described a visit he made to a dance hall named *El Salón* while in Mexico. He was struck by a curious arrangement whereby the orchestra played in the middle of adjoining rooms, separating the wealthier and poorer dancers. He recalled a sign in the poorer section: "Please extinguish your cigarettes, to avoid burning the barefooted dancers." "Is that where you heard the folk songs around which you built the work?" I asked. Copland smiled and admitted that he chose them from a collection of Mexican folk songs right here in America, "for their variety and usefulness as themes." In retrospect this fits in very nicely with reports about the theme-centered teaching methods of Copland's principal teacher, Rubin Goldmark, inherited in turn from his teacher, Antonin Dvořák, during the three years (1892–1895) the Czech master was teaching in New York.

El Salón México is typical of Copland's mature style, music drawn from folk song and jazz that gained a large public following and the respect of the critics. But by the 1960s he and Bernstein stood alone while many of the next generation of American composers fell under the spell of a particularly strict atonal version of the twelve-tone system—a central European import, born in part out of dark pessimism as World War I approached.

When I conduct the suite from Berg's *Wozzeck* or Schoenberg's *The Survivor from Warsaw,* two composers who established the twelve-tone method, I find myself using the same expressive gestures that I use for the passionate late Romantic music of Strauss, Brahms, and Mahler, their immediate predecessors. The notes may be strange but the emotional vocabulary—sudden accents, pressing sforzandos, portentous crescendos and diminuendos, and sliding portamentos—is familiar. Not only did a majority of American composers of my generation turn away from the remarkably vital and universally admired American school established by Gershwin, Copland, Ellington, and I must include the codifier of the language of jazz, Louis Armstrong; many of these composers stripped down the twelve-tone system to its mathematical core. As it turned out, by abandoning any hint of tonality and expressiveness, an entire generation of composers started losing the music-loving audience.

In his fifth Harvard Lecture, "Twentieth Century Crisis," Bernstein argues against the abandonment of tonality. He posits that the overtone series—a fundamental note, its octave, fifth, third, and so on—is everywhere in nature; in the human voice, in bird calls, "trumpeted" by elephants and sung by whales. This scale of nature is to music as is nature's prism, the spectral colors of the rainbow, to painting. Bernstein did employ the twelve-tone technique in *West Side Story,* in the rumble fugue, and in the second "Meditation" in *Mass* (borrowing an *eleven*-tone row from

Beethoven), but in every instance Bernstein's music is expressive, rhythmically catching and comes home, gravitates back, to a recognizable tonal center and a sense of closure.

Copland also experimented with twelve-tone techniques, "In my own way," in his *Piano Variations*. "I felt a need to change ... it forced me into a different more fragmented kind of melodic writing that resulted in chords I had rarely used before." I recently conducted the orchestral version of the *Piano Variations* and it is a highly emotional and powerful work. In his "Music for a Great City," Copland followed a stricter usage that produced a completely atonal work, with none of the charm and immediacy of his beloved folk-inspired music. I once overheard Lenny chiding Copland on the phone: "You, too, Aaron—going over to the other side?" Copland was, after all, the doyen of American music.

The last time I saw Aaron was at an airport. He was walking about with his ticket in hand. He looked lost. I ran to him. "Aaron, this is Maurice from Kansas City; you shouldn't be traveling alone." He recognized me. "That's all right. I'm trying to find the gate for Las Vegas, where I'm guest conducting." "What pieces are you playing?" He paused, searching, then he looked at me with his charming smile and that lovely bent-nosed profile—Copland encouraged solo winds to sculpt his themes with a profile—and said, "Don't ask."

Ben Udell

I have learned that despite the instinct to run, getting near someone in the throes of illness is as uplifting for myself as it may be for the one who is ill. In the Kansas City Philharmonic there was,

in this most Midwestern of orchestras, a Brooklyn-born timpanist, Ben Udell, a unique character who breathed cynicism and
yet was quite idealistic: "Truly beautiful ... Jewish but in a major
key!!!" wrote my poet wife, Gloria Vando. I was announcing to
the Kansas City Philharmonic that we, the orchestra, were going
to honor the first-ever Chinese cultural delegation to the United
States with a performance of a historic Chinese musical work,
when Ben, breaking all player/conductor/rehearsal protocol suddenly played a glissando on his timpani. Boing! "I'm not playing!"
he announced, in full Brooklyn talmudic singsong pilpul. "I'm not
playing because of the Chinese government's position on Israel."
Baiting me before the whole orchestra. Two Jews in a conflict.
What fun. "Intermission," I shouted as softly as I could and went
over to Ben to say something like, "Fine, don't play, but don't make
such a display. Please." You see, I respected Ben, and everyone
knew he was "different." There would be his refusal to go to New
York to play in Carnegie Hall on some other "principle."

Ben was stricken with cancer and had to be hospitalized. I
had been the music director at most four or five years, while Ben
had been in the orchestra for twenty years or more. You would
think there would be some musicians in the orchestra who would
visit him. Alas, Chris Gekker, a new young trumpeter he had
befriended, and I, his Jewish/musician connection, were the
only ones.

Ben spoke with me about Brooklyn, his kids, his poetry. I witnessed what may have been Ben's last *m'chiah* (blessed moment).
In the next bed to this small shrinking man was a powerfully
built bronze Adonis, all muscle and testosterone. The man was

carefully sponging, caressing is a better word, his dark beard preparing to shave. Enter his lady friend, a young curvaceous beauty, and Ben looked at me and spoke *in Yiddish, "Oi, s'fagen oigen"* (Oh my God, a pleasure for the eyes).

At his funeral, a quartet of string players from the orchestra finally decided to honor their colleague, but they got lost in a few places. I imagined a grinning Ben, laughing (*kveching*) at them from the open casket. I sat for a few last moments as the people started filing out, when I saw a young man walk down the aisle, get down on one knee before the casket, cross himself, and quickly slip a pair of shiny new wooden drumsticks out of his jacket and place them in the casket—Ben shouldn't go to heaven without a pair of sticks.

Katastrophe!

It was only a year later, in my sixth season with the Kansas City Philharmonic, that I blew a deep hole in my life. It took nine years to dig myself out. I brought it on myself, cutting free all the lashings that had held me in place. Goody-goody boy becomes ravenous with lust, freefalling into dark recesses, scraping away at passions I dared not imagine. I was drowning, and stopped holding my breath, wanting to see what was there, deep in the darkness. One day I was the celebrated "Man of the Year," the next, I was divorced and unemployed. No manager would represent me. With but two exceptions, David Amram and David Bar-Illan, all those who had been "avid" friends, who doted on me, were unavailable. I was *traif* (unclean). There were a few months of guest conducting engagements on my calendar, *Mass* at the Vienna State Opera, and two weeks with the Hong Kong Philharmonic ... then nada. My children were mostly estranged. I was in a fiery relationship that slowly turned to ashes.

It is difficult for a decision maker, a leader, to admit he was lost. With the help of Richard Streiter, a former student who became a close friend, I was introduced to a renowned psychiatrist, who, after hearing my story, spoke one word, "katastrophe," and accepted me as a patient. Over the next seven years Martin Bergman was the master navigator who helped me find safe shore, and guided me as I built a new career in American music, and as a professor. Slowly, I learned to forgive myself and earned my way back into the lives of my three beloved children, who were making their way in music and the theater. (See photograph 11.) Gloria remarried and built an enviable literary career: editor, poet, publisher, and feminist. In time she, too, would let me into her life again. I met and married a marvelous woman, Ellen Waldron, landscape designer and artist. She was my loving partner for twenty-two years, until pancreatic cancer took her. As I write, I sit surrounded by her beautiful perennial gardens in the Berkshires.

I have come to embrace my time with the Kansas City Philharmonic in spite of its awkward ending. One thing I have learned from Martin Bergman, there is no tabula rasa, no erasing the past. We carry it with us. It is "the story of our life" as Virgil said. Kansas City remains a crossroads, in earlier times the jumping-off point for eager settlers heading west, and the endpoint for Boston-based bankers and entrepreneurs to invest some of their assets. Virgil's "quarrelsome town" underscores this juxtaposition.

For my opening concert I reached high, Mahler's "Resurrection" Symphony. My mother, who was running a very sophisticated women's lingerie store on Madison Avenue, flew out. She had developed an eye for what we now dub the 1 percent, and at the after-concert reception, a lovely garden party in the home of Henry Block, founder of H&R Block, she came over to me to say, "Don't get too fancy, they're a bunch of farmers," meaning, play simpler music. She was offering fifty years of storekeeper's wisdom—stock the merchandise the customer wants. I listened. And for six years the Kansas City Philharmonic and I made lots of good music for the people. The orchestra's skill and range were on display for our East Coast concert tour to the Kennedy Center and Carnegie Hall in January 1977, and we earned excellent reviews. Carnegie Hall was a space I took for granted, but for many of the musicians—like our piccolo player Tom Hurst, who still calls me—it was the fulfillment of a dream.

I was slow to realize that Kansas City had a built-in inferiority complex. When it was announced that Bernstein would be coming to Kansas City for his sixtieth birthday festival, a high-powered New York public relations firm—retained by the Chamber of Commerce or city hall, I never found out—contacted me to control and maximize the story so that Kansas City was in-the-news, part of the national conversation. Kansas City was so busily comparing itself with other cities, so hungry for big-time visibility, it hardly recognized its own unique legacy in Charlie Parker, Thomas Harte Benton, Virgil Thomson, and a farmer who became our president, Harry Truman. I wish them well.

12

The Academic Life

♪

*I*n the fall of 1984, thanks to my old friend Howard Brofsky, I began my teaching at the Aaron Copland School of Music at Queens College. Howard was a brilliant musicologist and bebopper, and lifelong lefty, whom I met as a fellow trumpeter at NYU in 1948. Howard has been my good-luck charm. He introduced me to Gloria Vando in Paris in 1955, and thirty years later cajoled me into taking over the Queens College Orchestra, "helping out," for a year. At first I was disdainful—"those who can, do," et cetera. Then again, why not? It would give me a schedule, something musical to do, and I would earn some money.

When I began teaching it was hard to imagine getting *beyond* those Bernstein and music director years, when I was climbing my way up the maestro career ladder. Let's face it: I threw myself off that ladder, and brutally. Around the time I began teaching, I told Lenny I was *seeing a doctor*—New York-ese for ongoing sessions with a shrink. He answered, "It's about time." "Why didn't you tell me?" I implored. "Who can tell you?" Words of wisdom from someone who had been *seeing a doctor* for decades.

I was soon sharing my passions for music with eager and talented young instrumentalists and a few graduate student conductors, and they drew me out. Through a conscious analysis of what I had been hearing when working with great orchestras and master soloists, I was able to teach musicianship to my students. I taught them how to taper the ends of phrases in Mozart, and start growing the next phrase at the level they had arrived at: a subtle dynamic approach that creates an endless, singing line. I pointed out the inner metronomes in Beethoven scores, constantly repeated sixteenth or eighth notes in the inner strings that prevented rushing, and gave the noble melodies above "room to breathe." I trained young, eager brass players and timpanists to ignore "global" dynamics in classic works—when everyone in the orchestra has the same *forte* marked in their music—to play far lighter than the strings and woodwinds, especially those long-held notes that work best when played *fortepiano* (a strong entry and an immediate softening).

The Queens College Symphony had no players of string bass, bassoon, oboe, or viola; I worked with what we had, never losing sight of how the music should sound in the best of circumstances, and with some rescoring and a few "ringers," young professionals who joined us at the final rehearsals, I was able to deliver three or four respectable concerts a semester. Teaching conducting was another story.

I decided to treat my conducting students as Bernstein did me, as serious, semi-informed, apprentices. He had three assistants, so I had three assistants (Lenny-aping often shows up in my life). He shared openly what he was thinking, was sure or unsure about, what worked or didn't in rehearsal. It was natural for me to do the same. I insisted on perfect rhythm, even over perfect pitch, and made my young conductors sing or play the thorniest licks and phrases in Stravinsky or Copland until they got them right. We conductors cannot ask a musician in our orchestra to play what we cannot sing, or play on the piano, perfectly, ourselves. I made my young conductors aware of rushing or leaking ahead in faster music, or dragging in slower music, a problem common to young musicians, including my younger self. Best of all, I was not hungry to conduct every concert, and I turned the orchestra over to each conducting student for three or four weeks to prepare their own graduation concerts, with me as prime kibitzer.

My conductor training seems to have worked. My first conducting class graduated in 1986 and twenty-five years later they are music director of the Canadian National Ballet and professor at University of Toronto, professor/conductor at Brooklyn College and founding director of the Riverside Symphony, and a Hollywood conductor and orchestrator with twenty-four movie titles to his name including the endearing "March of the Penguins," for which he put on his composer's hat and wrote the original score.

I was not thinking about academic advancement when, after two years, my chairman asked if I wished to apply for tenure. I thought to myself, "Sure, why not?" Bernstein, and Aaron Copland, the school's namesake, sent letters of support. (When I called Aaron he remarked, "So there's a school named after me, how nice!") My tenure appointment, which went smoothly, was obviously based on my professional experience, not on advanced degrees. I wondered, was I cashing in my chips? By good fortune there were more chips to be earned, for a second career had begun.

13

American Music
The Re-Creations

♪

*T*hanks to the college I now had the financial security and free time to follow my eclectic American music muse, to quote Ellington, "music beyond category." Up to then, I had soft-pedaled my natural ease with American music, not wanting to be pigeonholed, but now I crawled into the hole on all fours. It started at a session with Doctor Bergman. Why, I do not know, but I said to him that the sixtieth anniversary of the concert that launched Gershwin's *Rhapsody in Blue* was fast approaching, and "wouldn't it be nice if someone would re-create that concert on the anniversary?" He paused, then asked, "Who would do a good job?"

Within days I reserved Town Hall for the afternoon of February 12, 1984, the exact day and time, and the exact block, West 44th street, of the original event. The concert was billed as "The 60th Anniversary Celebration of Paul Whiteman's Historic Aeolian Hall Concert." Gershwin's *A Rhapsody in Blue* was listed alongside other works by Zez Confrey and Victor Herbert. Luckily it was a

Sunday afternoon, a good day for seniors who carried nostalgia for the 1920s flapper era to venture out.

At the New York Public Library I found copies of the 1924 program and pored through dozens of reviews of the concert and started assembling the musical materials. Many of the original parts and scores including what was then called *A Rhapsody in Blue* were at the Paul Whiteman Archive at Williams College. Others I had to transcribe from close listening to vintage recordings, a process that also taught me respect for the magnificent musicality and skills of Whiteman's musicians. Re-creating the entire program was no small challenge. I felt a further responsibility to emulate the authentic performance movement: original instruments, tempos, size of forces, and especially performance style. In contrast to the Rennaisance and Baroque early music aficionados, there were recordings I could learn from. The archivist at Williams led me to two men still alive who had played in the original concert in 1924, and I was able to interview them. One was in a nursing home out west and had little to offer. But Milton Rettenberg, a pianist and a lawyer, who had grown up with Ira Gershwin and knew George well, had total recall for the music and personalities. He was the first to play the *Rhapsody in Blue* after Gershwin—I have his 1924 "arranger's copy" of the original piano score, signed by Gershwin. He lived not far from me in New York and he turned out to be an invaluable fountain of information.

I went liquid, cashed in all my stock, about $22,000 at the time, and proceeded to "produce" the concert. I hired a contractor, Herb Harris, a marvelous drummer who had once played a tour with Whiteman. Herb studied the 1920s recordings and put together a band of excellent studio musicians. I hired two fine pianists: the jazz stylist Dick Hyman to play the Zez Confrey group including "Kitten on the Keys," and the elegant Ivan Davis for the *Rhapsody*. I hired a publicist. His press releases garnered many preconcert articles and appearances on radio. The concert sold out, leaving hundreds of disappointed people on the street wanting tickets, and we got rave reviews. I recovered all that I had invested, and two days later the band, the soloists, and I boarded a plane for a six-day engagement and a TV show at *Teatro Sistina* in Rome, and where Italian audiences came dressed ą la 1920s with boas and white scarves.

I have done the concert many times since, and I believe that the secret of the program's success lies in the artful and inspired way Gershwin transforms the same ragtime and blues harmonies; the fiddle, brass, and sax colors; and the banjo, drum, and tuba rhythms that the audience had been hearing and toe-tapping to throughout the evening, into a masterwork with immediate appeal. My double life as a teacher, and my new mission unearthing and re-creating historic American music concerts, had begun. Philadelphia's Music Theater Festival hired me to reconstruct and be music director and arranger for Gershwin's 1927 Broadway show, *Strike Up the Band*. During our very successful run in the summer of 1984, I told them about *Queenie Pie* and they were excited at the idea of producing an Ellington premiere. With the help of writer/director George C. Wolfe, and Duke's son, Mercer—who allowed me to peruse Duke's sketchbooks where I found several excellent songs—we fully developed *Queenie Pie* in time for the 1985 season. And eleven years after Duke had passed, his last musical was produced, with the excellent authentic Ellington Orchestra in the pit. After we closed in Philadelphia, the Kennedy Center moved us to Washington for the fall season.

Carnegie Hall's Jazz Legacy Series (1989) was the capstone of my American music passion. I presented three reconstructions in a single week: Ellington's first appearance in Carnegie Hall (1942) for which he composed his signature concert work, *Black, Brown and Beige*; Antheil's outrageous 1927 *Ballet Mécanique* concert—everyone knew about it but it hadn't been heard in sixty-two years and it deserved and got a much-needed reevaluation; and a long overdue resurrection of the work of James Reese Europe, the first King of Jazz, with a lovingly played re-creation of his 1912 Clef Club concert, the first all-Negro concert in Carnegie Hall. These concerts gave me scholarly prestige in modern music and black music circles and led to several recordings.

Dvořák the Source

As I researched the materials of these historic concerts, Antonin Dvořák's name kept surfacing. And at the 1991 Dvořák Sesquicentennial Conference in America in New Orleans, I announced an irrefutable historic connection between Dvořák and three seminal twentieth-century American composers. Two of Dvořák's American composition students, Will Marion Cook and Rubin Goldmark, had in turn become the teachers of Duke Ellington, Aaron Copland, and George Gershwin! This shocked many American musicologists who had begun to espouse a revisionist party line, that Dvořák regretted his early enthusiasms for the significance of black music for the future of America's music.

Czech musicologists and musicians were ecstatic. I had uncovered such a rich connection to Dvořák's American legacy. Oxford University Press offered me book publication and I produced *Dvořák to Duke Ellington,* about "America's Music and Its African American Roots."

One sour note here: in a television interview in 1991 Isaac Stern declared his support for the demolition of the Dvořák House on East 17th Street by its new owner, Beth Israel Hospital; it was a landmarked brownstone where Dvořák had lived for three years and where he composed the "New World" Symphony, the "Humoresques," and the Cello Concerto. "We have the music, we don't need an old house," said the savior of Carnegie Hall. I had put no small amount of effort into staving off the demolition of the Dvořák House, organizing the support of prominent musicians Yo-Yo Ma, Bill Warfield, Wynton Marsalis; coordinating with the Czech and preservationist communities; giving a "Save the Dvořák House" concert in nearby St. Georges Episcopal Church. But Isaac's position and backing by the *New York Times* really helped turn the tide against us. The Dvořák House was demolished. But its loss inspired Jan Pokorny, a Czech-born architect and preservationist, to arrange with the Czech government to purchase Bohemian National Hall for one dollar. It was a huge abandoned building on East 73rd Street erected by the Czech community in 1896— Dvořák was among the donors then. Soon a planeload of skilled Czech artisans and workmen moved into the basement and began restoring and modernizing the building. The large bronze plaque that was mounted on the Dvořák House and the fireplace mantle from Dvořák's apartment were rescued and moved into Bohemian Hall, where a "Dvořák Room" dedicated to his American legacy was established. My Queens College Orchestra gave an inaugural concert in the beautifully restored ballroom; it turned out to have superb acoustics. We played Smetana's *Má Vlast* (My Country), six-tone poems based on Bohemian myths and peasant life, the most familiar being the flowing of the river Moldau through the countryside before emerging triumphant by the sacred old castle near Prague. There were many tears of joy that evening.

Josef Skrovecky

Josef Skrovecky, an early researcher of Dvořák's American adventure, and Czech lover of freedom, gave a magnificent keynote speech at the 1992 Dvořák in Iowa Centennial Conference, held at the University of Iowa. He spoke about the so-called lost provenance of the Negro spiritual "Goin' Home." Scholars all knew the music for "Goin' Home" had been adapted from the slow movement of Dvořák's "New World" Symphony, with added words by a former pupil. What could he tell us that was new? Skrovecky played recordings of several jazz settings of "Goin' Home" and wondered, "Were the jazz musicians, or even those that sang the spiritual, aware that it was a creation of Dvořák's [key word: creation] and what did that mean?" Josef spoke of his early days in World War II Prague playing jazz saxophone and writing. Under the Nazi and Communist occupation he and other young Czech writers could not get their (often radical) works published, but they continued to write plays and poems and stories, and passed their typed manuscripts or carbon copies, held together with a single staple, among themselves. Even after the front sheet with the title and the name of the author would tear off, the most interesting manuscripts continued being passed around and read. For Josef Skrovecky this was the height of honor; to create a work so worthy it had a life of its own—author unknown. In this way, "Goin' Home" became a "traditional," "anonymous" folk song. Skrovecky was postulating a profound notion. It inspired thoughts about creativity, authorship, mortality, the fragility of ego, the artist as messenger.

14

On the Road

♪

I soon became a frequent guest conductor in the Czech
Republic. Several of the concerts led to interesting adventures. For an all-Gershwin 100th anniversary concert
in Prague with the FOK Orchestra (Film, Opera, Koncert), I wrote
well in advance about the importance of finding a good banjoist
who could read music for the concert—I said I'd even settle for a
guitarist playing a banjo with guitar tunings; we'd miss the ringing open "clang" that the open tenor banjo tuning produces, but
at least it would provide a banjo color. When I arrived in Prague
and started rehearsing, there was no such player; there was an
empty hole in the music every time a banjo cue came up and
I could not hide my disappointment. During intermission, the
orchestra's personal manager came to apologize for the absence
of a banjo player. "There are plenty of banjo players in Prague,"
I said. "Just walk across the Charles Bridge and you'll find two or
three." "They can't read music," countered the manager. "Get me
one anyway; I can teach them most of the parts by ear." At the end
of the morning rehearsal the manager approached the podium.

"We think we have your banjo player. He is waiting for you at your hotel." "I can forgo lunch, let's walk to the hotel." At noontime you can get around "Prague center" much faster on foot than sitting in a limousine or a cab as it tries to work its way through the traffic and the labyrinthine, medieval, one-way streets.

We arrived at the Konvento, a four-hundred-year-old monastery that was converted into a hotel around 1900 when the art nouveau style was first emerging. The pale walls of cut stone, highlighted by occasional bits of exposed fresco, harmonize well with the clean, classic lines of the furnishings and quiet colors of the wall hangings.

A pie-faced, pleasant fellow in his midforties was seated at a corner table in the small dining room. There was a banjo case against the wall and copies of the Gershwin banjo music in front of him. He had a large cloth napkin tucked under his collar and was leaning forward, slurping his soup.

Speaking in Czech, the manager introduced me. The banjo player looked up and addressed us in perfect English. "My name is Simon Flesch. I am really a piano tuner." Back to the soup.

"That's good, at least you play in tune," said I, trying for levity.

"I'm a better jazz bass player than a banjoist." The soup again.

"Great! You know chords. If you want, I can write chord names into the parts, like a lead sheet. Why don't you take out your banjo, let me hear you play?"

"No," said Simon, as he pushed away the bowl and removed his napkin. "Let's just go to the rehearsal and see if I can do it."

"By the way," I asked, "where did you learn to speak such good English? Are you really Czech?"

Simon paused. He lowered his big brown eyes and smiled; pointing the huge soupspoon at me for emphasis, he said, "I'm all Czech … and all Jewish. Just like you!"

I had met my match.

As we walked to the Hall together, Simon loosened up and told me his story, how his family fled Prague for London when he was three, about his marriage to a Czech Christian woman in England and their return to Prague after the velvet revolution with their daughter, Leah, who is now a Hebrew teacher.

A chair and stand were organized for the banjo, between the first and the second violins, fairly close to the podium. I sat near him while the orchestra assembled, quietly singing the banjo parts and filling in the other instruments, as his finger followed the music. The oboe sounded the A. The afternoon rehearsal began.

Simon played perfectly. By the end of the session everyone in the orchestra understood why I was so insistent about the banjo. The little strummed E major arpeggio that introduces the slow theme in the original jazz band setting of the *Rhapsody in Blue* is a precious surprise to all who think they know the piece. I taught the orchestra to play straight eighths, ragtime style, rather than the anachronistic 1940s swing many orchestras use when playing early Gershwin. The banjo pumped away through the tuttis adding 1920s American spice. We sounded very authentic.

Touring China

If God is in the details, he/she has smiled on Shanghai. In June 2008, I discovered a cosmopolitan city, much of it walkable, yet there is greenery everywhere—flower boxes line the highways; even under the dark and dusty elevated roads there are plantings. Most streets are tree lined. Some tree trunks are wound with protective hemp rope, and most have their branches heavily pruned, French style, to keep them healthy and in check. There are block-long gardens everywhere, a quiet oasis for flying your kite above the tallest (often tasteless) new high-rise, or for strolling away from the busy streets. Waiting for traffic lights is made more bearable by a digital countdown of "seconds to go" before the light will change.

Then there is Pudong. When I first visited a dark and depressing Shanghai in 1980, we drove from the airport through Pudong, a boggy river island of farm fields reeking from night soil. Today it is an architectural wonder, a twenty-first-century city with beautiful riverfront walkways lined with curio shops and ice cream parlors. Slick-looking tour boats ply the wide Huangpu tributary of the Yangtze River, on the other side of which stands Shanghai's historic Bund—a collection of elegant late nineteenth-century banking houses. I visited at night and every building on both sides was lit. The contrast between the past and the present is striking, literally a "great leap forward."

Social interaction seems to exist on at least three levels. The old retirees I saw gathered in the pastry shop every morning, with marks of a life lived hard on their faces, babble away in Shanghainese, still dressed like the Mao generation with no apparent Western influence. Then there are the apparatchiks, everywhere—middle-class workers who dress Western but who interact within very formal lines; they bow, they rote-speak English phrases, and some gather in the style of a military muster, lining up to be addressed by an overseer. Finally there is the hip-hop, smartphone-carrying generation. Sassy girls with extreme makeup and couture hairdos share the sensibility with their spike-haired boyfriends. They wear knock-off designer label clothes and know all the pop-star lyrics, ghetto moves, and the latest movies, and they speak vernacular American English.

I was engaged to conduct the Shanghai Opera Orchestra. Compared with my first China guest engagement in 1990 their orchestras had improved immensely. Back then only the strings were acceptable. Woodwinds were erratic, brass players and tim-pani, unbearable. I remember spending the better part of thirty minutes tuning the four opening chords of Mozart's *Magic Flute* Overture, getting the octaves and fifths in order before adding the thirds, making the triads ring and shine. Everyone smiled at their success. At the next rehearsal we were back to square one; I had to give up. Over the next eighteen years the players began meeting what we in the West assume to be professional stan-dards. What helped the most was the return of Western trained players. In past decades they went off to Germany, Russia, the United States and never returned. In time there were more secure orchestra jobs waiting in China and teaching opportunities galore. And here I was, two decades later, doing Mozart again. I offered the very respectable opera orchestra some refinements: tapered phrases, reduced brass and timpani volume, and I brought along an effective set of bowings. Together we produced what our solo violinist said was "the best Mozart he ever heard in China." The parents of Tong Shen, my brilliant conducting student at Queens College, hosted me afterwards at an upscale restaurant.

Beijing is Los Angeles to Shanghai's New York: a car city with seven outer rings, and growing. Much of the same skyscraper frenzy as in Shanghai has produced a "crane index"—yes, they list the number of cranes up and working as if it were a stock market tally. My concert with the China National Symphony Orchestra fell three weeks before the start of the 2008 Summer Olympics. Beijing had been scrubbed clean; again there were colorful plantings everywhere. The new stadium, a huge, striking architectural work—knots of noodle-like girders support the span—is close to my hotel. But a fog of pollution started building up the Monday I arrived, and grew to a point by Friday where I could not see more than two blocks outside my window and the sun was completely gone. I was depressed. Then came Saturday morning, a sunny, clear, you-can-see-forever day, the day of my concert. The windows of the hotel were thrown open to allow in the fresh air. Of course the traffic and factories were on a weekend schedule, and this let the beauties of the city emerge. This is how the People's Republic would adjust for the athletes, and the world's TV viewers, during the coming Olympics. China never ceases to amaze.

I was leading the CNSO in an all-American concert. The orchestra, bigger than the one in Shanghai, read the music easily but it all sounded the same. They were quite attentive as I helped them create an American sound for Copland's *Appalachian Spring* and his Third Symphony, sculpting Aaron's open, out-of-doors intervals and swinging his folksy tunes. The audience was young and enthusiastic. The way they held their breath after the dramatic stop in Barber's "Adagio for Strings" told me they were very sensitive to music.

My Chinese book publishers came backstage to greet me and present me with the newly published Mandarin translation of my first book. I blanched; the English title on the handsome fold-around cover read *Dvořák to Duck Ellington*! The cover has since been reprinted.

The CNSO director, Guan Xio, who affected the appearance of a starving Parisian poet—red-eyed, chain smoking, unshaven, sloppily dressed—invited us all to a special restaurant in the inner ring. We were driven to the Forbidden City through the widest, cleanest street I have ever seen: Beijing's Champs-Élysées, its monumental buildings lit or framed by lights. The centuries-old traditional restaurant prepared a Chinese feast, with Western alcohol and Cuban cigars. The (translated) conversation was very real. Guan Xio, who composes works that join traditional Chinese singers and instrumentalists with Western orchestras, had just returned from a ten-day state visit to Sichuan province to experience the aftermath of a recent earthquake tragedy first-hand. He had been commissioned by the government to compose a "Requiem to the Children of Sichuan."

Guan Xio described the sadness, how in some towns an entire generation of school-age children had been wiped out. But he also was moved by the spirit of survival. I asked him to describe the form of his composition to come. He was quite eloquent. It will be in five parts: the calm of the countryside, earthquake, Dante's hell, the spirit of survival, and a tribute to a particular nomadic "nation" (there are over forty ethnic nations in China) that had all but been destroyed in the earthquake; they play a very sad music on a double bamboo flute, which he will feature in the work. There will be a chorus as well.

Back to the Foreign Experts Hotel in short order, obviously the leisurely ride along the "longest, widest road in China" had been planned. It was Sunday morning and the smog-ola was back.

15
The Road Ahead, The Academic Life II

♪

O n December 7, 2012, an article, "The Maestro of Flushing," appeared in the *New York Times*. I was about to lead the college orchestra and combined choirs, almost three hundred musicians, in a performance of Mahler's massive "Resurrection" Symphony in the beautiful Fifth Avenue Church of the Heavenly Rest. "Mr. Peress," the *Times* reported, "called it a heady undertaking at this ripe time in his career, one that has him reflecting on his own life and his relationship with his mentor, Leonard Bernstein, who loved performing Mahler, a fellow conductor-composer of Jewish origin."

The concert was for me one of those rare "count-on-the-fingers-of-one-hand" moments. The house was full, the acoustics both warm and razor sharp, the band played as if inspired, and I brought my full maturity to the task. The simultaneity of the concert and the *Times* article felt like a reaffirmation, a vindication of my decision twenty-seven years back, to teach; I hadn't given up real music making. Mahler helped.

At a time when other composers were searching for ways to move away from tonality and sought daring instrumental effects, Mahler created a musical universe that embraced and ennobled the past, paying homage to two hundred fifty years of Western musical development and thought. His meticulous performance indications—over three hundred sets of guiding instructions printed in the score of his Second Symphony and many more hundreds of markings above critical notes—reveal his own "received" approach to music making. Mahler plots out subtle, flowing adjustments of time, and demands fearless, extreme ranges of dynamics; "with the greatest unfolding of power," (sounds more convincing in German, *mit hochster Kraftenfaltung*), or my favorite Mahler instruction for very soft playing, "The composer thinks here, roughly, of the isolated sounds of a scarcely audible music, carried over by the wind [*von Wind vereinzeld*]." I always feel Mahler's hand on mine when I conduct him. These markings and instructions tell us how he must have performed the music of the great masters as well as his own.

By this time, my twenty-eighth year of teaching, the Queens College Orchestra had gradually grown in depth and quality. Thanks to our chairman, Ed Smaldone, who navigated the appointment of several stellar instrumental faculty members,[1] the college has been attracting talented students who help raise the technical and musical level of the band. Students came from all parts of the world as well as New York City. The word was out that the Aaron Copland School and its orchestra is "happening." A culture of excellence has established itself in the orchestra. At the beginning of a new term we get to work quickly. Students sitting in on their first rehearsal experience the band tearing through a new work at sight and realize they must get up to speed, and quickly.

The other half of my work at the college is instructing advanced conductors seeking a master's degree. Well over half of my thirty-five former students have conducting jobs with college and professional orchestras. Many stay in contact with me. As if to recognize how lonely is the life of the conductor, it has become apparent that for many I will forever be their mentor. I get panicky emails—"I just found out I have to conduct Beethoven's Seventh next week, anything I should watch out for?" And I email back suggestions about tempos and a very effective bowing trick I learned from Maestro William Steinberg, plus what I remembered from the Felix Weingartner book on Beethoven symphonies. Just recently I got an email from a former student who is starting a new university post—"Would you look over my ideas for programs?" To my surprise, he really needed help. Over a period of days we came upon a pair of programs that are well balanced and will instruct and engage his new students and their audience.

I was flattered to be invited to teach Twentieth and Twenty-First Century Performance Practice at the CUNY Graduate School. The doctoral students prepare modern chamber works of varying complexity for the class and I am expected to make suggestions and offer a critique, much like what I do when I conduct. But I wanted these students to gain an overview of the major trends, composers, and schools of the period, from the overemphasized, hegemonic

Second Viennese school to minimalism, from Bartok to Reich. We also covered the national schools that welled up over the century in Brazil, the Czech-speaking world, France, and America. I brought in my own scores of modern works, works I had performed that presented unusual challenges. George Crumb's *Ancient Voices of Children* called for Tibetan prayer stones that when squeezed as they are tapped produce taps that rise in pitch. One movement of the piece has two overlapping scores meant to be played simultaneously—the slower one, notated in an endless circular shape, was superimposed over a traditional horizontal score of a bolero-like ostinato. We studied Antheil's wild, piano roll–driven *Ballet Mécanique*; we studied the eclectic mélange of styles in Bernstein's *Mass,* and the all-but-lost 1920s ragtime style as applied to Gershwin's original jazz-band version of the *Rhapsody in Blue.* The students' term papers were revelatory; some drew elaborate timelines of the entire century; one student made a much-needed index for Ellington's *Music Is My Mistress.* I learned so much!

The Queens College orchestra began presenting unusual concerts in Manhattan venues. Our first celebrated the exact 100th anniversary of Dvořák's symphony "From the New World," December 12, 1993, with a performance at Symphony Space. We have been performing concerts of Czech masterworks every spring at the Czech Center. To commemorate Lincoln's bicentennial we performed Earl Robinson's *Lonesome Train* in the magnificent sanctuary of the Riverside Church, with three hundred singers and folk musicians; Ruby Dee was our narrator, and Sam Waterston spoke the voice of Lincoln. Robinson's folk-inspired orchestral works continue to have an immense spiritual influence on me.

L'chaim

I lost Earl, Duke, Lenny, David Bar Illan, and Malcolm Frager in my sixties. In my seventies and eighties, the first to go, the first shock, was Morton Gould, then one by one, the members of the Modern Jazz Quartet, and more recently Howard Brofsky. I have been to the Cathedral of St. John the Divine—the first time to honor the passing of Duke—to say good-bye to Virgil Thomson, Betty Allen, Alvin Ailey, and John Lewis. Their music holds my heart. My time will come; meanwhile, L'chaim, to Life. I live for my family *and* to make music.

I remember visiting Lenny while the New York Philharmonic was on tour in Denver. It was toward the end of my Kansas City days. I was starting a love affair that threatened to shake up my seemingly comfortable life and I must have been long-faced. "What's wrong?" he said. I shrugged but could not answer. "I know," he continued, "you're trying to figure out what to do with the next two decades of your life." A notion that I dared not examine at the time, but one he had obviously faced and dealt with. I thought of this story, not only my reaching out to an old trusted mentor, but for the need to face the reality of finite time and trying to take hold of it, carpe diem. When I was recently asked by a good friend to consider performing her friend's score, something I have been do-ing with an open mind all my life, I responded, "As to Ms. Albert's score, I am at a place where I struggle to choose between works I have grown to love that I will be conducting for the last time. . . . Just said good-bye to Dvořák Eighth; I am about to say farewell to the *Rite of Spring*. . . . I am scheduling *Mass* for next November. Sorry."

Stravinsky at Queens College

Stravinsky was not just joking when I encountered him in 1967 and he said, "There are more *wrong* notes than *right* notes in my *Rite of Spring.*" As I prepared for my "farewell" performances I consulted several revised and ostensibly *authentic* scores of the *Rite of Spring,* and realized that his cryptic comment was more than a play on words. One of my students brought in a facsimile of the manuscript and we visited every anomaly between the various editions with what he had originally written. Despite Stravinsky's quip, there are only minor differences; they all do justice to this masterpiece.

What does stand out is Stravinsky's splendid autography. Every stem is perfectly vertical, and of the same length, and connected to well-formed note heads ... until we get to the last two pages of the "Dance Sacral" ("Sacrificial Dance"), one of the thorniest rhythmic challenges for orchestra players and conductors alike, where every measure has another meter and there are few patterns one can rest upon. Several master conductors, including George Szell, avoid the work because of this. On the final pages of the facsimile, Stravinsky's perfect musical penmanship suddenly collapses; the stems lean drunkenly to the right and the note heads are ill-formed and float off, detached. The score—like the sacrificial maiden, possessed, dancing to her death—looks out of control, very much like it sounds; there is a sudden pause, and as the final notes trip off the page, she spills into the abyss.

Our second performance came off particularly well. I know what the students are capable of, and after we built the piece—in this case, for most of the students, their first *Rite of Spring*—I got up there and conducted as if they were a pro band, and tried to give them and the audience the full experience of our art. Being in the middle of, enveloped by, a live performance of the *Rite* was according to my fans and critics a deep twentieth-century musical experience. I was happy and proud.

Afterword
Music Is My Faith

As I write at eighty-four I am starting to understand why music sounds so clear, so right, in the hands of seasoned artists. I now seem to be receiving this gift. Age has worn away the superfluous and I am developing heretofore elusive music-making powers. I remember hearing trumpeter Dizzy Gillespie in his last years; in his prime he was best known for a blinding technique and thrilling high flights an octave-plus above the staff. His range had shrunk down to notes on the staff and below, but Dizzy's exquisite ear came into play. He examined the chords running beneath him and picked out unique lines and licks and spaced them perfectly, not unlike the exquisite brush strokes of a Tang Dynasty ink-wash master.

I now find myself controlling time rather than the other way around. I am finally able to fulfill every moment, etch every phrase, mark every rhythm to my satisfaction before moving on to the next. I can envision the middle and end, the profile and terrain, of many works, be they a four-minute overture or an hour-and-a-half Mahler symphony. These days when I study scores or mount the podium I am quite conscious of where I am in life and art.

There are those among my friends who bemoan the passing of the good old days. Bernstein famously once asked if the orchestra was becoming a museum, or a doomed dinosaur. This was in 1980, before the cyberworld roared in. At times I, too, bemoan the shrinking of the musical world I grew up in and the ubiquitous screens and phones people now live so much of their lives with. The eye has trumped the ear. But I am lucky to be working with young musicians. And I can report that the immediate connection I had with my father through music, and the epiphanies that converted me forever to make music my faith, are alive and well. There is no shrinking of the steady flow of applicants to conservatories and colleges to study music. Hundreds audition at Queens College every year despite the odds against ever making a living with music. When asked about this by an anxious parent, I wonder aloud—how many English majors write the great American novel? And imply that in fulfilling their musical selves, they master the immense discipline and attention to detail one must commit to bring a work of art alive at a predetermined moment in time. This prepares them for life and for many kinds of work.

There is also emerging a new "live" music life. Players are becoming entrepreneurial, forming odd, unorthodox ensembles. They take on catchy names. Everyone is a conductor at times. And they all write arrangements and compose new works for their group and in every conceivable style, mixing jazz, rap, rock, Schoenberg, and world music with computer-generated sounds. They find venues in bars and churches and comedy clubs and dance halls. They teach, play gigs, and have day jobs to support their music habit. They do their own public relations, create a following with the help of social media, and share their creations worldwide with similar groups, through the Internet. *Apres moi, la fantastique.*

Coda

My time in this world, my little wedge, and from where it derived, have occupied me, and you, my dear reader, if you got this far. Question: How did the dream inspired by *The Barrier,* my shining mission and hope for mankind, work out? Have I influenced others or have I been preaching to the proverbial choir? Have I used my art to serve or have I been tempted by vanity? Count me among those who lean left, who are for the people even in the face of Voltaire's truth, that both Evil and Brotherhood live side by side. I reaffirm liberal feelings; salute and embrace nature, the sun and the storm; and gaze stubbornly ahead, passing on what I think I know about the Art of Music.

When the time comes—my last breaths—will I recite a final Shema "God is one"? I don't believe in a God in whose name believers maim, murder, and burn books. I want to embrace *my* God—even the word has been spoiled—I want to embrace a oneness, Spinoza's pantheist Yahweh. On the other hand, when the time comes, will I succumb to some narcissistic need, wanting my thoughts, my doubts, to be documented until the last conscious second, as did British iconoclast Christopher Hitchens, his restless "Jewish after all" spirit adding some extra legitimacy to his outsider-ness? His ever fulsome mind amusing us, challenging us, holding our attention, shocking us, ad infinitum. I hung around through his last recorded bodily functioning second, admiring but empty-handed. He did not reveal, tell us about, *the end.*

I have a theory. I imagine myself passing through an ever-shrinking circumference of the cone of life. As the space narrows I become increasingly more insightful, and as I approach the apex, ultimate knowledge, complete wisdom and understanding, arrives for but a split second at the moment of death; defines, and is death … and it cannot be shared. Will there be music, Spinoza's pantheist symphony? I know that hearing is the last sense to go, and knowing this I sang and played for my dearest Ellen until the last second.

When at four in the morning the nurse told me that Ellen's death would happen at any moment, I reached for my trumpet, for Stardust, for bugle power, for the kissiness of lips and breath. I shoved a pillow in the bell and sang my heart out starting on D minor, the key of joy and sadness, of the Ninth and Mozart's *Requiem,* sang my heart out with "Lover Man":

> Someday we'll meet
> And you'll dry all my tears
> Then whisper sweet
> Little things in my ear
> Hugging and a-kissing,
> Oh, what I've been missing
> Lover girl, oh, where can you be?

Ellen and I enjoyed our small converted farmhouse in South Egremont, nestled among the majestic low-lying Berkshire

Mountains of southwest Massachusetts. (See photograph 12.) I still drive up there on weekends to enjoy the land, the quiet, her spring daffodils, and her generous gardens that arrive on time through the summer and fall. Last year I brought a bugle to South Egremont's Armistice Day ceremony, watched as the town fire truck, adorned with flags and bunting, led a small contingent of veterans in a short march from the firehouse to the town's modest memorial tablets. Several marchers, squeezed into a motley mix of old khaki uniforms, shouldered rifles. There were speeches and a prayer honoring the town's fallen soldiers. As the prayer ended, I surprised all present with a warmly phrased rendition of "Taps." Part of me was back in Camp Everett, back in my Boy Scout troop, a kid with a bugle, being for a moment the center of everyone's attention. The better part of me was keenly aware of the passing of generations and my need to join with the town's folk to honor that passing and my belief in the magic of the bugle's simple four notes of nature, the DNA of all the music I had ever known.

"I Go On"

It is late August 2014. In a few weeks I will be conducting the Bernstein *Mass*. As I study the familiar music and text, fresh and deeper insights surface. How Lenny came up with a compelling dramatic story—the loss of a beloved leader who gave us hope who is honored by a formal Latin Mass, at the same time a young street community asks tough questions as they search for faith—a compelling dramatic story that freed Bernstein to once and for all join his theater and symphonic music in common cause, and to join his searching Jewish soul with all faiths who seek peace. I remember him wearing a huge wooden cross during the final rehearsals of the premiere. The message is, alas, timely. In 1971 the quicksand of Vietnam dominated the news; now it is the Middle East.

There is a moment of calm toward the last part of *Mass* when the Celebrant realizes he is losing control of his followers. He is alone and fingers out a simple tune on the piano, "Our Father who art in heaven, hallowed be thy name," and sings along. A few clarinets and a guitar join to accompany him as he intones, "I Go On," his own credo, "I Go On ... to celebrate another day."

This is where I find myself, coping with this proud old body and health issues; the unquenchable call to live and love and make music never ceases. *L'chaim,* I Go On.

Notes

Chapter 1

1. Max Frankel, who went on to become the editor of the *New York Times,* had his bar mitzvah the same morning as mine. In his memoir, *The Times of My Life and My Life with the Times* (New York: Random House, 1999), he writes of how he sang all the required prayers. My memory may have been playing tricks for I always coveted the invidious notion that I sang—and to my joy the choir sang responses—and Max simply chanted.

Chapter 2

1. Valaida Snow (1904–1956) debuted on Broadway in 1942 as Mandy in Eubie Blake and Noble Sissles's musical *Chocolate Dandies.*

2. Ian McEwen, Interview, *New York Times,* March 31, 2005.

3. Claude Debussy, letter to Pierre Louÿs, January 17, 1896.

4. Langston Hughes, *The Weary Blues* (New York: Knopf, 1926).

5. From 1926 to 1939 Irving Mills managed the Duke Ellington Orchestra. He sang on some of their recordings and wrote lyrics to several songs: "Mood Indigo" (1931), "It Don't Mean a Thing if It Ain't Got That Swing" (1932), "Sophisticated Lady" (1933), "Solitude" (1935), and "Caravan" (1937).

6. "Something else Black Benny said to me came true—He said (to me), 'Dipper, As long as you live, no matter where you may be—always have a White Man (who likes you) and can + will put his Hand on your shoulder and say—"This is My Nigger" and Can't Nobody Harm Ya.'"(The peculiar punctuation is Armstrong's.) *Louis Armstrong in His Own Words,* edited by Thomas Brothers (New York: Oxford University Press, 2001), p. 160.

7. Walters opened the club in 1942 at 1580 Broadway at 47th Street in a

landmark three-story, wedge-shaped building that marked the north end of Times Square. Prior to Walters, the building was home to the Palais Royale with the Moulin Rouge in the basement in the 1920s. Norman Bel Geddes had designed the interior. Later it was occupied by the Cotton Club from 1936 to 1940 after it left Harlem.

Chapter 4

1. Jay McAllister, tuba; Alan Raph, trombone; Brooks Tillitson, horn; Gary Goren and me, trumpets.

Chapter 5

1. In 1938, the Nazi annexation of Austria (or Anschluss) forced Krips to leave the country. Krips (1902–1974) was raised a Roman Catholic, but would have been excluded from musical activity because his father was Jewish. Krips moved to Belgrade, where he worked for a year with the Belgrade Opera and Philharmonic, until Yugoslavia also became involved in World War II. For the rest of the war he worked in a food factory.

2. Brahms timings, thanks to Steven Ravioso: Gould/Bernstein, Sunday April 9, 1962; 25:49/13:45/13:47 [51:30]; Fleischer/Szell 21:19/14:36/10:53 [47:00]; Curzon/Szell 22:16/16:06/11:56 [50:00]; Serkin/Ormandy 20:25/12:45/11:14 [46:00].

3. New York: Farrar, Straus and Giroux, 1961.

4. Debussy said, "I should like to see a kind of music free from themes and motives or formed on a single continuous theme. The development will no longer be that amplification of material, that professional rhetoric, which is the badge of excellent training. But it will be given a more universal and essentially psychic conception." Oscar Thompson, *Debussy: Man and Artist* (New York: Tudor Publication, 1940), pp. 102–103, quoting from André Fontainas, "Mes Souvenirs du Symbolisme."

5. Bartok was conscious of a constant proportion, 0.618 evidenced in nature and the human form, and built his movements so that they reached their most dramatic moment when they arrived at, or around, six/tenths of their length.

Chapter 6

1. Sigmund Freud, *Der Mann Moses und die monotheistische Religion: Drei Abhandlungen* (Amsterdam: A. de Lange, 1939).

2. Mark Edmundson, *The Death of Sigmund Freud: The Legacy of His Last Days* (New York: Bloomsbury, 2007).

3. As of this writing the hall has been renovated three times and another is being planned.

Chapter 7

1. Lynn Garafola, ed., *José Limón: An Unfinished Memoir* (Middletown, CT: Wesleyan University Press, 2001).

Chapter 8

1. Google: AMG AllMusic Guide: Pop Artists: Paul Gonsalves.

2. We arrived at Piano Concertos #2 in B-flat, #4 in G, and #1 in C for the first concert, and #3 in C minor, and #5 in E-flat, for the second. Clearly, key relationships were the determining factors and Brendel chose wisely. In the first concert moving down a third, B-flat to G, creates an expectant mood. Thence going from G to C, the classic dominant/tonic resolution, produces a sense of closure. The second concert is all in three flats, going from C minor up a third to E-flat, an uplifting move, and to Beethoven's key of choice for triumphal works.

Chapter 9

1. Ray DesRoches, percussion; Karen Phillips, viola.

2. In the early 1930s Morton Gould, a child piano prodigy with no stopover at a music academy, became an eighteen-year-old staff member of Radio City Music Hall and the WOR Mutual Network. He worked his way up from popular duo-pianist to music director/composer/arranger/conductor for a weekly show, "The Cresta Blanca Hour," for which he composed snappy commercials as well as his celebrated "Symphonettes," short movements based on folk

and popular music for a studio orchestra and dubbed them his "Light Works." "Serious Works," dozens of commissions, for the San Francisco, Chicago, and New York Philharmonic orchestras, and the New York City Ballet followed. He was a fine conductor who recorded with the Chicago Symphony, the New York Philharmonic, and an orchestra organized under his own name. When he died in 1996, practically with a baton in his hand, he was the doyen of American composers, recent president of ASCAP, with an active catalogue of over one hundred compositions.

3. Baldwin recruited me when I left the Philharmonic and since Bernstein and my close friend David Bar Ilan were Baldwin artists, I signed on. They set me up with "loaner" pianos throughout my career. I still have my last "loaner," sold to me at a going-out-of-business price the year they went under. When I needed (seven!) concert grands for my Carnegie Hall re-creation of Antheill's *Ballet Mécanique,* Baldwin was only too happy to please.

4. "Maurice, that's just beautiful. . . . Your essay brings back memories to me. Bravo to you. You captured the time and how I was then—not an easy task. I am most grateful. Much love, and thanks, John." (Email to author, December 1, 2012.)

5. Almost forty years later Dr. Bob Lombardo, once a fellow trumpeter at NYU, came to my performance of *The Marriage of Figaro.* We met afterwards and he told me that he played pop concerts with the Chicago Symphony when he was in medical school and that one day he got a panicky call from Herseth: "I have to play a jazz piece by Ellington at Ravinia next week and need you to show me what to do. Can we meet?" Bob's coaching on the "Suite from *Black, Brown and Beige*" may well have contributed to Herseth's mastery of the style.

Chapter 10

1. Allen excited much attention for her portrayal of the title heroine in a concert performance of Arthur Honegger's *Judith,* the work with the American Concert Choir and Orchestra under conductor Margaret Hillis at Town Hall. Critic Edward Downes said of her performance, "Allen sang the music of the first two acts without apparent effort. Her voice had a rich, true mezzo-soprano quality with a brilliant top, and dark reedy chest tones. It was so beautifully

placed and focused that it gave the impression of being larger than it was. Her piano and even pianissimo singing had the velvet quality that carries so beautifully through an auditorium. She was a figure of regal dignity, yet she showed dramatic temperament, too" (*New York Times,* January 15, 1957). Her staged opera performances included Joplin's *Treemonisha* and Virgil's *Four Saints in Three Acts.*

2. The American Composers Orchestra tribute at the Plaza Hotel, fall of 1986.

Chapter 11

1. Meryle Secrest, *Leonard Bernstein: A Life* (New York: Alfred A. Knopf, 1994).

2. The Stieler portrait belonged to the Hinrichsen family, owners of Editions Peters, a music publishing house that dates back to the time of Mozart. The painting had been moved to America when the Nazis arrested and killed several family members and seized the Jewish-owned firm. Only a few younger relatives were able to escape. And thanks to the Nelson-Atkins art restorers, the cheerful portrait with vivid colors now resides in Bonn, Germany, Beethoven's birthplace.

Chapter 15

1. Daniel Phillips, Marcey Rosen, Morey Ritt, David Jolley, Charles Neidich, Michael Lipsey.

Index

About the Author

Maurice Peress leads an unusual American musical life. Born to a Baghdadian father and Polish mother, his first music was Arabic and Yiddish songs. He grew up in New York's Washington Heights, became a busy dance band and symphonic trumpeter, and was drafted toward the end of the Korean conflict, landing him in a newly integrated Negro Regimental Band. Here, Peress shares what he learned as an assistant to Leonard Bernstein with the New York Philharmonic and symphonic arranger for Duke Ellington. He worked closely with icons of the concert and operatic world—the five piano concertos of Beethoven with Alfred Brendel, Tristan in concert with Eileen Farrell—as he led orchestras in Corpus Christi, Austin, and Kansas City, and as a guest conductor in Chicago, Prague, and Shanghai.

With insightful writing, Peress brings us closer to a wide array of boundary-crossing American works and musicians he has worked with: Feldman's Rothko Chapel; Ellington's Black, Brown and Beige; Bernstein's Mass; Antheil's "Ballet /"; Whiteman's Birth of the "Rhapsody in Blue"; Earl Robinson's Lonesome Train; David Amram; Langston Hughes; José Limón; Francis Ford Coppola; Aaron Copland; John Corigliano; Benny Goodman; the Modern Jazz Quartet; and more.

Peress explores an enormous range of American works and musicians. He walks us through the bitter musicians' strike in Kansas City, and he is not shy about weaving aspects of his personal life—loves and losses—into the story: his fall from grace in his fifties that found him starting a fruitful academic career at the Aaron Copland School of Music and his Jewishness— "being a member of the first generation when it was OK to be Jewish."

In his first book, Peress explored America's music and its African American roots. In *Maverick Maestro,* a musical mission emerges, a lifelong commitment to "give concerts that reconstruct delicious mixed marriages of music, black and white, Jazz and classical, folk and concert, Native American and European; works that bring people together, that urge us to love one another."

Maurice Peress is the author of *Dvořák to Duke Ellington* (Oxford University Press). He teaches at the Aaron Copland School of Music and guest conducts in the United States and abroad.

For Product Safety Concerns and Information please contact our
EU representative GPSR@taylorandfrancis.com Taylor & Francis
Verlag GmbH, Kaufingerstraße 24, 80331 München, Germany